Twayne's English Authors Series

Sylvia E. Bowman, *Editor*

INDIANA UNIVERSITY

Edward Dowden

 TEAS 148

Edward Dowden

By KATHRYN R. LUDWIGSON

The King's College

Twayne Publishers, Inc.   ::   New York

Preface

The problem challenging anyone making a study of Edward Dowden is his failure to support the Irish Literary Renaissance that was taking place when he was at the peak of his literary power. Despite the many volumes of his critical essays, Dowden wrote neither an essay about the Renaissance nor a critical study on the works of its chief representative, W. B. Yeats. Since Dowden appeals quite persistently to a particular view of life and literature in defense of his position, one would suspect that, underlying his actions and defense, is a system of thought, the application of which would explain his aloofness from the Irish literary movement.

The discovery and analysis of such a system of thought and its application to his life and works provided the incentive for this study in its initial stages, but early research revealed Dowden's outstanding philosophic insight into modern human experience, a world-view that endeavored to bridge the gap between the validity of poetic knowledge and the empirical assertions of scientific materialism by a Transcendental dialectic that would be true to both. This viewpoint not only determined his relations to the Irish Renaissance but also provided a mythic interpretation of life for his poetry and became the basis of his esthetic theory. The strict honesty of his viewpoint, its faithfulness to the human condition, and its intelligent, early diagnosis of the times should make Dowden a literary critic as relevant today as he was to the late nineteenth century.

Preliminary to the study, Chapter One relates what little is known of his life. Dowden once wrote to Elizabeth Dickinson West: "I applaud the prudence and discretion of choosing what we think best for the world and exercising a strict discretion, leaning towards the side of leaving little rather than much." When she became his second wife, she applied the statement literally, preserving only those portions of his personal letters to her—the chief source of biographical information concerning him—that she thought worthy and burned the remainder. Since most of his major publications are no longer in print and therefore not easily accessible, Chapter One also provides a descriptive analysis of these works.

Chapter Two traces the unifying concept of Dowden's world-view in its scattered references in his criticism and poetry. Dowden's view, like Thomas Carlyle's in England and Ralph Waldo Emerson's and Henry David Thoreau's in America, becomes a persuasive expression of the continued impact of the Transcendentalism inherited from Romantics William Wordsworth and Samuel Taylor Coleridge, who were, in turn, influenced by the German Transcendentalists. The implications of this world-view on Dowden's esthetic theory is the subject of Chapter Three. His early struggles to gain a consistent viewpoint in his criticism, as it is recorded in his greatest work, *Shakspere: A Critical Study of His Mind and Art,* appears in Chapter Four. Attempting to assimilate into a harmonious world-view and esthetic theory both the scientific Positivism, increasingly prevalent during the Victorian era, and the Transcendentalism inherited from the Romantics, Dowden found his view placed on trial by Shakespeare's seemingly strict positivist approach to life. And Chapter Five examines the application of Dowden's viewpoint as it motivates his reticence to encourage or contribute to the Irish Renaissance. The controversy between him and those advocating pure Irish literature reveals a divergence of opinion much more complex and philosophical than at first recognized by his opponents.

Because the goal of this study is limited to an analysis of Dowden's literary theory as it motivated his criticism of authors and their works, little attention is paid to his political activities, which, because of materials available, could become the topic of a separate monograph.

Acknowledgments

I wish to express my gratitude to Mr. William O'Sullivan, Keeper of Manuscripts at Trinity College, Dublin, for the information and help I received; to Mrs. Lennox Robinson, Hester Dowden's daughter, the only living relative of Edward Dowden, who lent me notes, discussed Dowden's character with me, and gave me permission to quote from his works, both published and unpublished; to Professor H. O. White, now deceased, recent Professor of English at Trinity College, Dublin, and former student of Edward Dowden, who gave me information; to Professor Frederic Faverty, who encouraged this study; to the librarians of National Library, Dublin, and Bodleian Library, who helped me find materials; to Professors Arnold Fox and Arthur Holmes, who offered many valuable suggestions.

I am indebted also to the following publishers for permission to quote: to Rupert Hart-Davis for two extracts from *The Letters of W. B. Yeats;* to Harvard University Press for two extracts from *Letters to the New Island* by W. B. Yeats; to the Moray Press for an extract from *AE* by William Clyde; to St. Martin's Press for four extracts from *W. B. Yeats: 1862–1931* by Joseph Hone; to Macmillan for six extracts from *Irish Literary Portraits* and two from *A Memoir of AE,* both by John Eglinton; to the Cambridge University Press for an extract from *F. D. Maurice and the Conflict of Modern Theology* by Arthur Ramsey; to Clonmore and Reynolds for an excerpt from *W. B. Yeats Letters to Katharine Tynan;* to Michigan State University Press for three extracts from *William Butler Yeats* by Morton Seiden.

KATHRYN LUDWIGSON

Contents

Contents

Chronology

1843   Edward Dowden, born in Cork, Ireland.

1859   Matriculated at Trinity College, Dublin.

1864   *Considerations on the Criticism of Literature,* publication of his inaugural address given as president of the Philosophical Society.

1866   Married Miss Mary Clerke; professor of English, Alexandra College, Dublin.

1867   Professor of English, Trinity College, Dublin.

1875   Introduction, *The Prose Works of William Wordsworth,* edited by A. B. Grosart.

1876   *Shakspere: A Critical Study of His Mind and Art; Shakepeare Scenes and Characters* (Dowden uses both spellings, *Shakspere* and *Shakespeare); Poems.*

1877   *Shakspere Primer; Studies in Literature.*

1879   *Southey* in the "English Men of Letters" series.

1881   Edited, *The Correspondence of Robert Southey with Caroline Bowles;* edited, *Sonnets* by William Shakespeare.

1883   Edited, *Passionate Pilgrim.*

1886   *The Life of Percy Bysshe Shelley.*

1887   Awarded LL.D. by the University of Edinburgh.

1888   *Transcripts and Studies;* edited, *The Correspondence of Henry Taylor.*

1889   Taylorian lectures on literary criticism in France at Oxford University.

1890   Edited, *Lyrical Ballads.*

1892   Edited, *The Poetical Works of William Wordsworth,* seven volumes; lectures on Elizabethan Romance at Oxford University; Dowden's wife died.

1893   Edited, *The Poetical Works of Percy Bysshe Shelley.*

1893–   Clark lectures on the French Revolution and its relation-
1896   ship to English literature at Cambridge University.

1895   Edited, *Poems by Robert Southey; New Studies in Literature;* married Elizabeth Dickinson West.

1896   Lectures at Princeton University on the occasion of its sesquicentennial (Clark lectures of 1893–96 revised and added to); awarded LL.D. by Princeton University.

1897   Edited, *Poems of William Wordsworth: A Selection; The French Revolution and English Literature; A History of French Literature.*

1900   *Puritan and Anglican.*

1904   *Browning* in "The Temple Biographies" series.

1905   *Montaigne* in the "French Men of Letters" series.

1909   *Milton in the Eighteenth Century.*

1910   *Essays Modern and Elizabethan.*

1911   Visit to Quebec.

1912   Edited, *The Ring and the Book.*

1913   Died on April 3. *A Woman's Reliquary* published posthumously.

1914   Published posthumously: *Fragments from Old Letters,* two volumes; *Poems,* enlarged edition; *Letters of Edward Dowden and His Correspondents.*

CHAPTER 1

A Part of the Whole: Life and Works

> . . . no spiritual thing can ever be completed. It is an atom of a growing whole; and its virtue lies in the vitality, not its completeness.—Dowden, *Fragments from Old Letters*, I, p. 25. The hairs on the tadpole's nose or the "Doctrine of the Enclitic *de*" and "*Hoti's* business," an invisible force urges men to expend their lives for these; and shall I doubt it is Something above and beyond themselves working through them as his art works through the poet.—*Ibid.*, p. 114.

I *Family Background and Education*

THE greater part of his life Edward Dowden spent studying and writing in his sunny room, eventually lined with twenty-four thousand of his beloved books, the spoils of many a rewarding adventure to the bookstalls. The son of John Wheeler Dowden, a merchant and landowner of upper-middle squireen tradition, Edward was born in the outskirts of Cork, Ireland, on May 13, 1843, the youngest of four children. Dowden, an old name in Ireland, appears among the principal families in the country towards the close of the sixteenth century; and it appears certain that the first Irish Dowden was a soldier of Oliver Cromwell who settled in southern Ireland and was given land there. The early Dowdens settled in Cork and became prominent citizens, every generation from the first settler there owning land. Regarding the three Cornish choughs ennobling the Dowden coat of arms, "Three draper's measuring-yards would have been more suitable," remarked Edward Dowden in later years; for Dowden's father had become a successful linen draper in St. Patrick's Street,

Cork, a business carried on by him until his retirement in old age.

Both of Dowden's parents were highly esteemed in the community because of their goodness and the charm and intelligence of their conversation. The mother belonged to the Presbyterian Church, the father to the Anglican Church of Ireland, and each parent reflects, respectively, his or her Scottish and English heredity and Protestant commitment, and, we might also add, each one's consequent influence in shaping the mature political commitments of their son. Writing to Elizabeth Dickinson West in later years, Dowden called his father the "best man I know, living really for others, most simple in his own habits and thoughtfully applying what he spares on himself (i.e. a great deal) to helping forward this or that person, in secret very often."

Edward's uncle Richard, once mayor and city librarian of Cork, was an ardent admirer of Wordsworth. Inspired by the great Romantic to a rare appreciation of the beauty of nature, this uncle awoke in his young nephew a comparable enthusiasm for the natural beauty of the countryside and an intense interest in the great poet. A love for the flaming rhododendron, the furze and heather glow of the hills, the open sea, and the miraculous sky never left Edward Dowden. Years later, for refreshment and recreation during college recesses, Dowden drifted with his family into the wilds west and south of Dublin; during the summer recess he especially enjoyed the seashore, where he loved to swim. During the spring recess he always tried to get away from the city to hike in the hills to enjoy the young greenery of spring: wood sorrels, primroses, violets, wood anemones, spurge in the woods, golden gorse, and leaping streams gladdened his spirit. And as the impact of Wordsworth was noticed in the uncle's book, *Walks After Wild Flowers, or The Botany of the Bohereens* (1852), so was it echoed in the later prose and poetry of the nephew.

Wordsworth's attraction for Dowden, basic though fluctuating throughout the years, was the power of Wordsworth's vision and the spiritual truth of his imagination. In Wordsworth, Dowden discovered the dual unity so admired by himself and so expressive of his own viewpoint. Sensitive as his mind was to the influence of his uncle's Wordsworthianism, however, not all the uncle's ideas impressed him. It is a fact, not without irony, that his uncle was also an active Liberator and supported the platform of Daniel

O'Connell, the founder of Irish nationalism—a political ideology utterly divergent from that which Edward himself later vehemently espoused.

Most of Edward's early education was acquired privately at home from his parents and tutors, a system he evidently greatly appreciated; for he later insisted that his own children be educated at home. Much of the time during his early years he spent reading and studying in the Old Cork Library—the only place in Cork that he remembered somewhat nostalgically in later years: "There is not much to see in Cork. The one thing I look back on with satisfaction is the Cork Library. I don't think Dublin has any collection of books so much read by a miscellaneous public of persons of quality, tradespeople, priests and parsons. It contains from fifteen to twenty thousand volumes, with greasier covers and more thumbed pages and more numerous pencil marks than those of any library I know." [1]

For a year Dowden studied Greek and Latin in Queen's College, Cork, as a nonmatriculated student. At sixteen he entered Trinity College, Dublin, under the tutorship of his cousin, Dr. George Salmon, later provost of Trinity College, Dublin. Here on the ground floor of Number 17 in Botany Bay Edward shared rooms with his older brother John, afterwards Bishop of Edinburgh. Here, too, Edward distinguished himself as a student by obtaining the highest honor in metaphysical studies, the Wray Prize, awarded as the result of competitive examination of the Senior Sophisters to encourage metaphysical studies. He also won the first-class Moderatorship in Logic and Ethics and the Vice-Chancellor's Prizes for English Verse and Prose Composition, a list of honors quite unprecedented in the history of the college.

The combination of a native intelligence and a captivating ability to express himself won Edward the admiration and respect of his fellow classmates; and, when he became active in the undergraduate Philosophical Society, he was elected its president. The address given on his inauguration into office was published later as *Considerations on the Criticism of Literature* (1864), a work astonishingly mature in its grasp of the fundamentals of critical theory which were to be the guiding principles of his later work.

As far as Dowden was concerned, the function of literary criticism is twofold: to appreciate and to analyze. Appreciation means to him the personal involvement of the literary critic with the literary product in the Wordsworthian manner, an involvement at once passive and active, the eye of the critic not only passively perceiving but also actively conferring on the work of art its appreciation. Dowden assumes that excellent art is informed with universals—goodness, beauty, and truth. The true critic, he maintains, would be able to demonstrate how the work is in harmony with the universal laws or tendencies of the human mind. The apprehension of what is good, beautiful, and true by the critic, both an intuitive and rational faculty, would enable him to point out how far the work "is born from the bosom of the Real." Such appreciation can be cultivated by the critic chiefly by deepening his love and "feeling-with-ness" for his fellowman and nature. In fact, the conditions of true criticism dwell in the soul of man—in a "loving heart and a loving eye."

But the critic should be able not only to *appreciate* but also to *analyze* good literature. His function as an analyst is twofold—philosophical and biographical—to ascertain, first, the various concurring causes which contribute to the total effect on the reader and to discover, second, what circumstances of the time, locality, or individual genius influenced the writer at work. Analysis so followed, Dowden affirms, leads to the discovery of principles in the philosophy and the history of literature.

In 1863, after Edward had received his Bachelor of Arts from Trinity College, he considered entering the ministry in London. Though already prepared by the Divinity School at Trinity, he did not take orders because of his serious doubts about the genuineness of the Bible and his lack of "a religious standpoint." He was strugglnng with the claims on his soul pressed by the German Romantic philosophy, especially by Schelling's objective idealism, and by Comtian Positivism. He used to say to H. O. White, one of his outstanding students and his successor to the Chair of English Literature at Trinity, "All that I want of being a clergyman is the hands of a Bishop on my forehead." [2]

Edward was gradually moving away from religious orthodoxy with its belief in a special revelation to a position which saw in both nature and man a progressive revelation of the divine-human. His eventual disavowal of the Christian faith is recorded in two sonnets:

In the Cathedral

The altar-light burns low, the incense-fume
Sickens: O listen, how the priestly prayer
Runs as a fenland stream; a dim despair
Hails through their chaunt of praise, who here inhume
A clay-cold Faith within its carven tomb.
But come thou forth into the vital air
Keen, dark, and pure! grave Night is no betrayer,
And if perchance some faint cold star illume
Her brow of mystery, shall we walk forlorn?
An altar of the natural rock may arise
Somewhere for men who seek; there may be borne
On the night-wind authentic prophecies;
If not, let this—to breathe sane breath—suffice,
Till in yon East, mayhap, the dark be worn. (Written after 1876.)

Memorials of Travel: V. On the Sea-Cliff (In Ireland)

Ruins of a church with its miraculous well,
O'er which the Christ, a squat-limbed dwarf of stone,
Great-eyed, and huddled on his cross, has known
The sea-mists and the sunshine, stars that fell
And stars that rose, fierce winter's chronicle
And centuries of dead summers. From his throne
Fronting the dawn the elf has ruled alone,
And saved this region fair from pagan hell.
Turn! June's great joy abroad; each bird, flower, stream
Loves life, loves love; wide ocean amorously
Spreads to the sun's embraces; the dulse-weeds sway,
The glad gulls are afloat. Grey Christ to-day
Our ban on thee! Rise, let the white breasts gleam,
Unvanquished Venus of the northern sea! (1873)

In the first sonnet, the religious exercises in the cathedral are expressions of a "clay-cold Faith" within a "carven tomb"; there is less opportunity in the cathedral to discover "authentic prophecies" than in the great out-of-doors where, even if natural revelation of divine mysteries should fail, one could at least breathe "sane breath." In the second poem, the same figure of sculpturesque coldness appears and is symbolical of the deadness of the Christian religion as compared to natural religion. Christ, a "grey Christ," "a squat-limbed dwarf of stone," deserves to be banned;

but Love, inherent in nature itself—in the birds, flowers, ocean, sun, dulse-weeds, and gulls—is to be the white-breasted nourisher, the unvanquished queen of life. Dowden believed the Christianity expressed in his day to be impervious to natural joy and love; as such, it was a dwarfed dead religion ("ruins of a church"). It promised life ("miraculous well") and salvation ("saved this region fair from pagan hell"), but it acted instead as an authoritarian creed ("the elf has ruled alone"). Because such religion had turned its back on the power of the universal love as manifested in nature ("unvanquished Venus"), it was outdated. The objection to Christianity implied in these two poems is radical: Christianity as practiced by the contemporary churches of Edward's day is described as a cold and lifeless form when contrasted with the life-giving powers inherent in nature.

A friend of the Carmelite College told Dowden that "an old Ursuline nun showed him a bit of verse copied into a blank page of her breviary—by whom she did not know—but she said, 'Poor man, I hope he is happy, and I remember him in my prayers.'" [3] The scrap of verse happened to be by Dowden, and it was most likely one of these poems. In the years subsequent to the writing of these poems, however, Dowden modified his radically antagonistic attitude towards organized Christianity due, in part, to the influence of Miss Elizabeth West, the dean's daughter, and possibly of John Dowden, his brother, Bishop of Edinburgh. Even so, Edward's detachment from the churches of his day, whether Anglican, Roman Catholic, or nonconformist, persisted until old age. While vacationing on the Atlantic seacoast at Castegoland in 1906, he was attracted by an old ruined chapel which became visible on an island during spring tides. Worshippers with their beads, kneeling and praying, would go round this chapel, from end to end, hurrying away before the tide reversed. Detachedly, Dowden remarked: "We heretics—who never go to church—have looked on, sympathizing, and sometimes the last of the devout have to wade with lifted garments through the incoming tide." [4]

As a result of his changing views, Edward abandoned the ministry and decided to study for a Master of Arts to prepare for a teaching career. The degree was conferred in 1867. The year previous to his graduation he had married Miss Mary Clerke, whose father, a landowner near the village of Skibbereen in West Cork, was descended from the family of de Hyde, who were distantly linked to the Royal House of Orange. For some undiscoverable reason, Edward's family opposed the marriage, though it seems to have been quite congenial and happy. Dowden loved children, and the three children born to him in the succeeding years—Hester, Richard, and Hilda—brought him great joy.[5]

II *Professor of English*

Dowden's first teaching position was in 1866 at Alexandra College, a girls' college in Dublin. There in the lecture room he met Elizabeth Dickinson West. The intelligent and talented daughter of the Dean of St. Patrick, she was his "best pupil." An ardent friendship, supplemented by an intimate correspondence, sprang up between them; and about the year 1872 Dowden realized that she was essential to him. It is a rare achievement "to love a woman without a single thought of the difference of 'he and she,'" Dowden himself recognized, "and profane men would deride such love as this." [6] In the view of a contemporary, "the situation can best be understood in the light of the idealism of Robert Browning, which reigned over it. Browning clearly taught that in every man's life there is one chance of salvation, through a woman." [7] Miss West undoubtedly became "The Haven" of Dowden's life, as described in his poem by that title:

> It was not love, but o'er the array
> Of maiden faces clustering there
> My glance careered, which well might stay,
> For this was frank and that was fair,
> No haven for my sail that drove,
> No pharos, sunniest isles I passed;
> Then suddenly—it was not love—
> The haven and an anchor cast. (no date)

"From the spirit of man to the spirit of man flow forth the issues of life and death," Dowden wrote later in *Studies in Literature*, a statement especially suitable in suggesting the circumstances of the long friendship between himself and Elizabeth Dickinson West, with whom he corresponded for about thirty years and whom he married in 1895, three years after the death of his first wife. Miss West had, in the interim, become a familiar guest in the Dowden home, was chosen by Mrs. Dowden as godmother to a son Richard, became "Aunt Bess" later to the children, and edited many of Dowden's essays and books. She was a keen scholar whose criticism Dowden respected.

She had published a study on Browning in *The Dark Blue Magazine,* "Browning as a Preacher," some sections of which Dowden appropriated with modifications for his biography of Browning; and he had acknowledged her influence in his lectures. Moreover, Miss West first suggested to Dowden that his Shakespeare lectures were worth publishing; and this publication, *Shakspere: A Critical Study of His Mind and Art,* brought him world renown. The two volumes of his letters to her, published by her after his death, form the most intimate record of his spiritual biography. These two books, however, are unfortunately limited in their value by excessive excisions, the necessity for which one cannot determine.

An understanding of the spiritual affinity of the two, however, helps measure the greatness of her influence. They worked as a team in publishing: Dowden edited her translation of Goethe's *Iphigenia in Tauris;* and after his death, she edited a second, enlarged edition of his *Poems* and aided in the publication of *Letters about Shelley,* edited by R. S. Garnett. The sincerity of Dowden's deep appreciation for her lifelong friendship is felt in the tone of the quotation he chose as a dedicatory tribute to her in his book, *Puritan and Anglican:* "To E. D. D. 'Truly, for my own part, if I were as tedious as a king, I could find it in my heart to bestow it all on your worship; yea, an 'twere a thousand pound more than 'tis.' "

One cannot help wondering whether Dowden's deep veneration for womanhood derived, in part, from his long friendship with Miss West. The homage he pays to womanhood is akin to worship, and he seemingly sees in womanhood a clearer manifestation of the Divine Love than he finds in man: "If a woman could put her hand in firmly and tenderly among the roots of our deepest life, and deal with our spirits truly," he wrote in a letter (Oct. 9, 1885), "well, we should not need much other gift or grace from God." Much like Auguste Comte, an early influence, he believed that the love of a woman could be such a supreme event that it would "interpret the secret of existence which divides the clouds of custom, and give a higher meaning to the whole of life." [8]

This exalted idea of womanhood he externalizes in his poem,

"The Heroines," in various personages such as Helen of Troy, Europa, Atalanta, and Eurydice. Even his interpretation of Goethe's *Iphigenia* is colored by this belief. As Goethe worked on the subject of Iphigenia, Dowden believes the great German master became increasingly conscious of the likeness of his own past to that of Orestes. As Orestes had been delivered from the Furies and then restored to calm and sanity by a sister's love and faith, so Goethe had been nobly influenced by Frau von Stein. "The sacred influence of a noble woman to soothe, to appease, to control, to elevate, to free—this is one motive of the poem," Dowden affirms in an unpublished lecture on Goethe.

In July, 1867, Dowden resigned his position at Alexandra College to fill the newly created chair of English literature at Trinity College in the University of Dublin, a position which he occupied for forty-six years. Few professors could equal either the eloquence with which Dowden charmed his students or the fervent belief in humankind with which he inspired them to achieve their best selves. "I can still recall the distinguished presence, the noble brow, and the mellow, golden voice," wrote H. O. White. "Coming to that classroom as a callow Freshman, it seemed as though a new heaven and a new earth were unfolded before me. The history of human culture was presented as a vast landscape, shimmering with the divine colours of a Turner, and lit by a light that never was on sea or land." [9] "Our saint of culture," John Eglinton, a younger contemporary of Dowden's, affectionately named the genial professor who was more interested that his students learn from literature about how to live mature lives than about how to become critical scholars. When Dowden's exemplary scholarship inspired his students to do penetrative, analytical research of their own, he was troubled lest he had failed to get across the "one thing needful." The mechanics of scholarship as an end in itself, uninformed with moral or spiritual value and therefore sterile, was to be avoided.

In Dowden's early notes written towards the writing of a poem, he wrote, "A palimpsest my soul, scribbled over by the world, but underneath the great hand of God." One might almost say that the whole of his life and work was directed to help his students catch a glimpse of the divine image impressed, not merely upon his own soul, but on life itself as demonstrated by the lives and works of the authors he taught. The students came to his home regularly in large numbers for many years on Sunday afternoons when he conducted open house. There were students of his, later scattered in all parts of the world, with whom he corresponded frequently; for he delighted in maintaining with them an almost parental relationship. Thirty of his students left Trinity College, Dublin, to occupy chairs in universities throughout the world. W. Macneile Dixon, author of *The Human Situation*, was one of these students; and another distinguished student who attended Dowden's classes in 1894, Professor Charles Marie Garnier, wrote an appreciative study of him in the *Revue Anglo-Americaine* (1928–29).

From the outset of Dowden's career as a university professor, he combined publishing with teaching; and he became increasingly better known, especially to the editors of various British literary journals, who solicited his critical essays for their publications. His articles and reviews began to appear in the *Contemporary Review*, the *Fortnightly Review*, the *National Review*, the *Atlantic Monthly*, and the *Nineteenth Century and After*. His chief work, as a matter of fact, was as a prose writer; but the fact remains that, had it not been for the necessity of providing an extra income to support his family, he would have made verse his vocation in life. It was verse, he said, that expressed his most essential self. And in the late 1860s he was exchanging verses and letters of verse criticism with other Irish poets: J. B. Yeats, Edwin Ellis, John Todhunter, and Aubrey de Vere.

Edwin Ellis, along with J. T. Nettleship and J. B. Yeats, had formed a sort of brotherhood of artists along the lines of the Pre-Raphaelite Brotherhood and had settled in Bedford Park, Cheswick, a village built by Norman Shaw as a reaction to Victorian bad taste. In 1869, J. B. Yeats had written that the brotherhood "abhorred Wordsworth," a letter which Dowden took seriously—altogether too seriously according to W. B. Yeats. Dowden, fired with the dogmatism of youthful conviction, beseeched the brotherhood to reconsider its position: few losses, he argued, can be greater than to lose the power of Wordsworth's genius. Ellis sought to assure Dowden that the brotherhood was by no means unanimous in its disapproval of Wordsworth's poetry; in fact, Ellis himself assumed the sole responsibility for the attitude of the brotherhood towards Wordsworth, especially of Yeats's attitude.

The opinion Yeats held about Wordsworth, Ellis explained, was "greatly the result of my holding forth to him on the subject with Wordsworth in my hand to draw examples from. With no other member of this supposed non-existent body of men have I discussed the subject at all, or heard them discuss it with each other." [10] After a visit with the group in London the following June, Dowden dropped the controversy.

During 1869 the poetry of Walt Whitman first attracted comment from Dowden. Dante Gabriel Rossetti had recommended to Dowden an edition of Whitman; and Dowden, along with Algernon Swinburne, endorsed the recognition and thus became among the first to recognize the genius of the great American poet. So enthusiastic was Dowden, in fact, that he published a short article on Whitman as the poet of democracy of his era, and he later read selections of Whitman to the Fortnightly Club at the university, but not without some apprehension about his audience's reaction, as he admitted to his poet-friend, John Todhunter. [11]

A strong personal friendship was formed by Dowden with Whitman through an interchange of letters, newspapers, and books for over a decade; and, when Whitman was in financial distress, Dowden was among those who campaigned for his relief. Whitman's friend, John Burroughs, with an introduction from Whitman, paid Dowden a visit. But Whitman's reputation was already in a grievous state, chiefly because of his "Calamus" poems; and, when Dowden, in his enthusiasm for the American bard, presented a copy of *Leaves of Grass* to Trinity College library in 1882, it was promptly returned to him by the librarian. In addition, the college threatened the local bookseller that it would withdraw its patronage if he sold *Leaves of Grass*. "Better also withdraw *Areopagitica*," retorted Dowden in his diary (Oct. 26, 1882).

On the eve of the publication of Dowden's article for the *Contemporary Review* on "The Poetry of Democracy: Walt Whitman," it was withheld and appeared instead in the *Westminster Review*. When the article was reprinted later in Dowden's *Studies in Literature, 1789–1877, The Spectator* (June 15, 1878) reviewed it with contempt. *John Bull* magazine (April 27, 1878) regretted that such an accomplished critic should fall a victim to the absurd culture of Walt Whitman. The Trinity College librarian and the journalistic critics misunderstood Whitman, Dowden judged, because they failed to relate Whitman's great works to the milieu of which he wrote.

III   *His first book:* Shakspere:[12] A Critical Study of His Mind and Art

In the spring of 1873 Dowden wrote the series of lectures to be given the following year on eighteen Saturdays beginning in February—"The Mind and Art of Shakspere," lectures which were to become the first draft of his book. He had been reading intensively in Shakespearean criticism, especially in German criticism; indeed, Dowden was at this time undoubtedly the most outstanding authority on German Shakespearean criticism. His lectures capitalized on the revival of interest in Shakespeare in the theater and in the press that had been stimulated, in part, by the New Shakespeare Society, reestablished in England in January, 1874, under the leadership of F. J. Furnivall. In the first year of its reestablishment, the New Shakespeare Society claimed four hundred and fifty members in its London and branch societies. Shortly after its inauguration, the branch society in Dublin numbered seventy members; and Dowden was one of its vice-presidents. "There is a tide in the affairs of men, / Which, taken at the flood, leads on to fortune," Shakespeare wrote; and Dowden was one of those wise men who, though they are themselves in the midst of the tide, rise above it by seizure of the opportunity which it affords. Dowden's lectures on Shakespeare attracted such overflow audiences that his class was moved temporarily from Alexandra College, where the lectures were scheduled to be given, to a larger lecture room of the Divinity School of Trinity College.

Dowden proceeded in his *Shakspere* as a biologist would treat a living organism: he studied the soil on which the organism grew, and then he carefully examined and analyzed the organism itself. He examined first the milieu of the Elizabethan age in which Shakespeare was born; and, having done that, he demonstrated how Shakespeare's dramatic art corresponded with the philosophy of Francis Bacon and with the theology of Thomas Hooker. From the Elizabethan age, Bacon, Hooker, and Shakespeare acquired the gift of devotion to fact: they had learned how to root their ideality in actual, concrete fact. Since a detailed account of Shakespeare's struggle against forces in his nature that opposed fact appears in Chapter Four, additional analysis of Dowden's *Shakspere* is delayed until then. Dowden's book was published in sixteen English editions and in a number of foreign translations, among them French, German, and Russian.

Dowden's lectures on Shakespeare behind him, he concentrated his studies during the summer of 1875 on the poets of his century, especially, as he said, on those who had captivated his attention and enthusiasm ever since he was a boy—William Wordsworth, Walt Whitman, Percy Bysshe Shelley, John Keats, Lord Byron, Victor Hugo, Alfred Tennyson, Robert Browning, and Arthur Clough. Thinking that these nineteenth-century poets might be judged from new points of view, he proposed to publish studies of them; and toward this end he had been lecturing on them during the school year of 1875. For a beginning, he wrote the Introduction to the three-volume *Prose Works of William Wordsworth* (1875). He was temporarily distracted from his pursuit, however, by a proposal from Macmillan for a *Shakspere Primer* for the series "History and Literature Primers," edited by J. R. Green, which was published subsequently in 1877. F. G. Fleay, prominent Shakespearean scholar, was surprised that Macmillan advertised Dowden's name for the *Shakspere Primer* instead of his since he seemingly had had a previous arrangement with the publisher; but Dowden, apparently knowing nothing of the previous arrangement between Fleay and Macmillan, accepted the publisher's offer.

The purpose of the primer was to guide the youthful student through the mass of Shakespeare literature. The primer, therefore, summarized the extent and results of the latest Shakespearean researches; it described briefly, but clearly, the features of Elizabethan London; it laid out the chronological order of Shakespeare's works as determined by internal and external evidence; it discussed the character, purpose, and general classification of the works as indicative of the stages of the mental and artistic growth of their author; and it presented the interpretation of Shakespeare's plays by various actors on the stage. Dowden also examined the verses closely to determine the chronology of the later plays, especially those verses selected by Fleay, who in 1874 had proved to the New Shakespeare Society in London that Shakespeare had only gradually introduced into his works double endings, Alexandrines, and short lines. This invaluable *Primer* was accepted for a long time as the standard summary of Shakespearean scholarship, and it appeared also in foreign editions.

IV   *Adventure in Poetry*

On October 10, 1875, Dowden's second daughter and fourth child was born. His responsibilities to be a breadwinner increasing, he kept on submitting literary articles to scholarly journals—"hack work," as he called it, that was necessary to supplement his salary for his growing family but that deprived him of time to pursue his first love—writing poems. It is a truism that poetry seldom has enriched its authors by royalties, yet Dowden never wholly abandoned it; and a small edition of his poetic efforts was published by Kegan Paul in 1876, entitled simply *Poems*. A second revised edition, published a year later, was destroyed almost completely by a great fire at the publishers in London.

Dowden's poetry reveals the sensuous but spiritual region of his soul—the deep, almost mystical, feeling for external nature—which found its best expression in poetry that is, to a great extent, Wordsworthian. When reading some of his finest sonnets, in fact, one could think that one is reading Wordsworth. Dowden's inspiration, like Wordsworth's, comes largely from Nature—free winds, open heavens, sweet hillsides—and, in Dowden's particular case, from rolling seas, "low sympathetic whisperings of a soul which holds communion with Nature." His intense desire to "feel with" every phase of nature is almost, like Wordsworth's, a mystic's longing to blend with the primal element of Nature, especially with sea and mountain. But Dowden goes beyond his master in coping with problems of later origin, and among these are evolution, democracy, human progress, and Eastern mysticism.

Wordsworth is not, however, the only noticeable influence on Dowden's poetry. His poetry also reflects Keats's rich, sensuous desire for earthly beauty—a reflection especially observable in his sonnets "In the Garden" and "From April to October," and in his "Ode to Beauty." In his Keatsian-Shelleyan poem, "The Skylark," he consciously compared the effort of the two poets; for the characteristics of the two are too obvious to be accidental. His poetry also manifests the influence of Tennyson. In the graceful and expressive poem, "Heroines," Dowden uses Tennyson's manner of telling Classical myths in the form of carefully constructed monologues in blank verse. The speakers are Helen of Troy, Atalanta,

Europa, Andromeda, and Eurydice. His own efforts at a compromise between Romanticism and Realism attracted him to Robert Browning, and he recognized Walt Whitman as the giver of a great spiritual mysticism that had the power of elevating man's heart beyond the sensuous experiences of life.

Dowden's poems are lyrical throughout, and the cry of the soul expressed is distinctively his. One finds in his poems a commitment to belief in a Divine Presence inherent in both man and matter and yet transcendent to both. There is a perpetual passing beyond the visible sights and sounds of earth into a mystical Presence. When Dowden is alone in his observation of the beauty of Nature, he is lifted to a participation with the Eternal. Of its reality, he had no doubt; but he did not know what to call it—Soul of the World? Life? Light? Love? Immortal Powers? Primal Force? Law? God? His mystical reactions are expressed in the following excerpts from his poems:

> With sea and sky, of powers I stood aware unowned of sense,
> Presences awful, vast, and uncontrolled.
> > "Memorials of Travel: III. The Castle (In Scotland)"

> Down upon you I sink, and leave myself,
> My vain, frail self, and find repose on you,
> Prime Force, whether amassed through myriad years
> From dear accretions of dead ancestry,
> Or ever dwelling from the source of things;
> In adulation vast and unperceived,
> Down upon you I sink and lose myself.
> > "Among the Rocks"

This belief is the strong fiber of thought that binds the poems each to each, and yet it is made up of odd strands—at once pagan, Christian, anti-Christian, Transcendental, mystical, and Comtian.

Such an agglomerate of strands appears little more than an unsettled electicism on Dowden's part; and to such insight, Dowden himself assented, at least in part. Yet he attests that by careful analysis one can discover in any poet a unified vision of life:

The happiest moment in a critic's hours of study is when seemingly by some divination, but really as the result of patient observation and thought, he lights upon the central motive of a great work. Then, of a sudden, order begins to form itself from the crowd and chaos of his impressions and ideas. . . . From each single work of a great author we advance to his total work, and thence to the man himself—to the heart and brain from which all this manifold world of wisdom and wit and passion and beauty has proceeded. . . . Taking the chief themes with which literature and art are conversant—God, external Nature, Humanity—we may inquire how our author has dealt with each of these. What is his theology, or his philosophy of the universe? By which we mean no abstract creed or doctrine, but the tides and currents of feeling and of faith as well as the tendencies and conclusions of the intellect. . . . And alike in this and in what we have termed the psychological methods of study, we shall gain double results if we examine a writer's works in the order of their chronology, and thus become acquainted with the growth and development of his power, and the widening and deepening of his relations with man, with external Nature, and with that Supreme Power, unknown yet well-known of which Nature and man are the manifestation.[13]

Assuredly, one must assume that Dowden included himself among the authors whose views of life can be discovered. For the present, however, this comment must suffice since a complete analysis of Dowden's world-view is the subject of the second chapter.

Also in 1876 Dowden arranged the explanatory texts accompanying *Shakespeare Scenes and Characters*, a selection of fine German steel engravings by distinguished Munich artists. Accompanying each engraving is an appropriate text from the play illustrated, some general views suggested by the play, and examples of the different schools of Shakespearean criticism. The book is unusually interesting not so much for Dowden's presentations of Shakespearean criticism, which are, after all, available more fully elsewhere, as for the collection of German engravings, which are governed by concepts of art that contrast with those of the English of the era.

V *Critical Lectures and Essays*

During 1877 Dowden wrote and organized his lectures and essays on nineteenth-century authors for publication by Kegan Paul: *Studies in Literature*, the realization of a dream envisioned as early as 1874. There were three types of literary criticism current in the 1870s: principle-oriented, which started with the principles by which a work is measured; description-oriented, which simply described or reflected the subject; and philosophy-oriented, which sought to discover the subject's opinion on points which appeared important to the critic. The criticism of Dowden is largely a combination of all three, but he seemingly believed that he was writing criticisms that were chiefly philosophy-oriented.

In *Studies in Literature* one sees Dowden apply his critical theory to a number of nineteenth-century authors and to at least four chief literary movements of the eighteenth and nineteenth centuries. In the first three essays, he points out that the four chief movements in the eighty-eight years under study were the evolutionary and democratic, the Transcendental, the scientific, and the Medieval. Except for the Medieval, each movement is not only noted but discussed at some length along with selected literary exponents of each. One notices some overlapping of authors since Wordsworth, Coleridge, and Shelley, for instance, figure as exponents both of the revolutionary and democratic and of the Transcendental movements. One discovers that Dowden judges both authors and movements by certain principles at the same time that he analyzes the philosophical orientation of the authors to God, man, and the universe. One is apt to find, however, that Dowden develops from the authors ideas that are more his than theirs.

What Dowden approves in the French Revolution with its related literature is its emphasis on the human intellect, its recognition of human brotherhood, and its concern with social progress. Here were a movement and authors who understood the intellectual and social ideals of the day. Any literature to be great, Dowden states, should reflect every vital influence of the period in which it was written. Thus, the early works of Wordsworth, Coleridge, Shelley, and much of Byron tend toward being great literature insofar as they are influenced by the revolutionary tendencies of their day. But the revolutionary movement and these Romantic authors who were inspired by it stressed excessively the abstract concepts which motivated the revolution—justice, equality, and brotherhood—and, like Shelley, treated them apart from their historical and social responsibilities. Too reckless, also, was the emphasis of the English poets on individualism, as in the case of Byron. Dowden adjudges as empty and sterile any concept, creed, or action which remains insubordinate to the historical and social order.

What Dowden sanctions in the Transcendental movement is its acknowledgment and enlargement of the spiritual life of man and its exaltation of material life by its belief in an immanent Divine Presence. The Transcendentalist chiefly to whom one is indebted for such deliverance and enlargement is, to Dowden, F. D. Maurice, who, more than his predecessors Coleridge and Wordsworth, kept a firm grasp on concrete reality. Dowden's sympathies, however, are not so heartily with the Transcendental movement and its idealistic basis as with the scientific movement and its empirical methodology; but either one, if it ignores the truth of the other, would be deficient. Dowden is troubled lest Transcendentalism, with its emphasis on the ideal element inherent in the universe, cause one to depart from the empirical facts of life by distorting or wholly replacing them. His chief objection resides in the faith-reason dichotomy. He distrusts imagination inspired by faith only, which he understands as characterizing the Transcendentalists; he prefers, instead, imagination inspired by reason as evidenced by authors who incorporate the scientific movement into their works.

Like *Shakspere: A Critical Study of His Mind and Art, Studies in Literature* was accompanied by public appreciation of Dowden's scholarly contributions. As an acknowledgment of Dowden's challenging service to the college community and of his inspiring contributions to the literary world, especially in the field of Shakespearean criticism, the Royal Irish Academy awarded Dowden a Cunningham Gold Medal—an award that stemmed from an old bequest which had fallen into desuetude for some time, but was revived in 1879 with the giving of four medals, one for mathematics, one for natural science, one for numismatic work, and one for literature. In 1879, Dowden was elected to the council of the Notes and Queries Society of Liverpool, a society cooperating with the New Shakespeare Society, whose purposes were the formation of a Shakespearean library, a concern for architectural restoration, and the discussion of art questions of current interest. The Notes and Queries Society became a social medium for the criticism of books, pictures, music, and plays; and of all of these Dowden was a fine connoisseur.

Frequently, Dowden's friends found the dignified professor at art sales, concerts, or the stalls of booksellers. The collecting of literary rarities—old books, manuscripts, and curiosities—became a form of recreation to him: "In this he felt the keen zest of a sportsman. This was his shooting on the moors, his fishing in the rivers." [14] He prided himself, for instance, on the discovery of several rare manuscript pieces by Andrew Marvell, Sir John Denham, and the Earl of Rochester which had interesting variations from the printed texts. Perhaps one of Dowden's rarest finds was a copy of Shelley's "A Refutation of Deism." In old Patrick Tighe's "little hole" in Anglesea Street, he also found an original uncut copy of Shelley's *Epipsychidion* and an original of Matthew Arnold's *Empedocles on Etna,* which had been withdrawn from circulation by Arnold.

Dowden, also a fine connoisseur of art and music, owned etchings and reproductions of Rembrandt, E. Burne-Jones, and William Blake. He delighted to pass around the classroom some of his rare finds—his priceless Blake sketches or a stack of early Wordsworth editions or a portrait of Dorothy Wordsworth from a private plate from which only twenty-four copies were taken. Great artists are the subjects of a number of his poems, and critical comments on artists and musicians color his letters.

VI *Biographies:* Southey *and* Shelley

After the publication of *Studies in Literature,* Dowden, at the request of John Morley, began writing a biography of Robert Southey for the "English Men of Letters" series; and this book became the first of four book-length biographies that he wrote, the others being *Shelley, Browning,* and *Montaigne.* Although Dowden would have preferred to write about Coleridge, Aubrey de Vere strongly urged Southey, Sir Henry Taylor offered the use of hundreds of Southey's letters, and the British Museum loaned a great volume of Southey's letters. By the late summer of 1879, Dowden had completed most of the research on Southey; and the book was published later in the year. The biography is indebted throughout to the Reverend C. C. Southey's *The Life and Correspondence of Robert Southey* (1830) and to J. E. Warton's *Selections From the Letters of Robert Southey* (1856). After reading the ponderous six-volume biography of Southey by his son, Dowden's concise little work of two hundred pages is a refreshing re-

lief. Seven editions of the biography were published in England
and America within the next three decades, and it was adopted in
1885 as a textbook by a college of India for native students preparing for examinations in English literature.

As a by-product of the Southey study came the edition of *The
Correspondence of Robert Southey with Caroline Bowles,* which
Dublin University Press published in 1881. Southey had wished
that Caroline Bowles's and his letters might ultimately be published; but Mr. Wartey, Southey's son-in-law, who had planned to
publish them, had died before he could accomplish the project.
Instead, Dowden took up the task, corresponded with Southey's
daughter, and edited the letters. The letters published were a
mere selection from the ones exchanged by Southey and Miss
Bowles from 1818 until her marriage to him in 1838. Since there
was already in print a large portion of Southey's correspondence,
this new edition could be justified only by its inclusion of warm
personal anecdotes of Southey's life and thought. By relating
much of what Southey thought, Dowden was able to capture
Southey's inmost being. The edition has two curious appendices—
first, a warm correspondence between Shelley and Southey, consisting of five letters that relate to the question of whether or not
Southey wrote an article in the *Quarterly* that had bitterly criticized Shelley's character and, second, a tabulation of Southey's
troubling, extraordinary dreams, which adds a certain psychological interest.

Southey and the *Correspondence* have, however, a deeper motive than that of ordinary biography; for Dowden presents
Southey in an attractive light, not as the celebrated poet laureate
of England for thirty years, but simply as a man of strong and
noble friendships and affections, an exemplary moral ideal. Dowden's biography of Southey, is, therefore, a written testimony of
his belief that the biographer's duty is to probe deeply within his
subject and endeavor to define the inmost life discovered there.
This art of the biographer, if faithfully practiced, would lead to
the discovery of the living moral law present in the life story. But
the biographer was not to use his discovery as a text from which
to moralize; rather, he was to present the moral law thus evident
as "part of the natural history, part of the physiology of his book."
The living law to be discovered from Southey's life Dowden regarded to be his self-discipline: Southey's great self-regulation—

his use of reason and will to control youthful emotions—was to be admired and emulated.

Dowden's edition of *The Sonnets* of William Shakespeare also appeared in 1881, in "The Parchment Library." Dowden's was the only edition of the sonnets with notes explaining their relationship to each other and to Shakespeare. In this work, Dowden devoted fifty pages to the history of criticism of the sonnets; he had accepted the division of the sonnets into two groups, those addressed to a young man who is the poet's friend and those to a dark woman who at first captivated the poet and then his friend—in other words, Dowden acquiesed to the common belief that the sonnets are autobiographical. Though Dowden does not profess to throw light on the identity of "W. H.," of the dark siren, or of the rival poet, he opines that "W. H." is the "Will" of the sonnets, that possibly he is William Herbert, Earl of Pembroke, and that the rival poet is perhaps George Chapman. The chief item of interest is Dowden's discussion of the sequences of imagery and idea in the series as the sonnets are commonly printed. Here, as elsewhere, Dowden's concern with the relation of the imagination to empirical facts shows itself. He observes, as he had in *Shakspere: A Critical Study of His Mind and Art* and as he later does in *Essays Modern and Elizabethan*, that all the enduring poetry of the Elizabethan age "was born of the union of heart and imagination," that imaginative feelings and real experience fuse in the poetic achievement.

The year 1882 saw the start of a correspondence with William Bell Scott of London, a friend of William Rossetti for thirty-four years, who sent Dowden a book of poems to review. Scott was the only one of Rossetti's old friends who managed to keep in communication with him through the last decade of his life, when he was deeply depressed. But, more significantly, 1882 was the year that Dowden received a proposal from Sir Percy and Lady Shelley, communicated through Sir Henry Taylor, to write an authoritative biography of Shelley, a work which Dowden completed five years later. This endeavor again brought him in contact with Rossetti, who lent Dowden his own research and his publication on Shelley, *Autobiographical Writings on Shelley*.

Dowden's invitation to write a biography on Shelley interrupted his study of Goethe, about whom he had been gathering materials slowly but steadily since the early 1870s. To fulfill his purpose, he collected Goethe books in German, French, and English; and he had carried on a course of reading for over a decade. In March, 1880, he wrote to his brother John that he had been "hankering" after Goethe for a long time, that he was preparing to give six public lectures in Dublin beginning on April 10, and that he hoped to make his study of Goethe's life and words his magnum opus.

The outcome of Dowden's Goethe lectures, delivered at Trinity College for the mutual benefit of its students and the ladies of Alexandra College, was rather startling and unexpected: Dowden was labeled as a rather dangerous threat to and corrupter of the youth of Dublin. "The Archbishop and his clerical posse sat on me," he wrote later to his brother, "and condemned me for contumacy to be racked, disembowelled, burnt." [15] In the lectures, Dowden presented Goethe as a pronouncedly non-Christian liberator from traditional morality and from an "indefinite idealism" through a return to Nature "to commune with the forces of the external world and also to consult the oracle in our bosom." But the reaction to the lectures turned out to be a veritable storm in a teacup, "a groundless clerical scare"; for the offended persons were not the authorities of the college or university but the clerics who had misunderstood Dowden's position. Although Dowden was far from theologically orthodox, he had a great respect for the traditional morality and was by no means disposed to call it "Philistine."

Even if the writing of the Shelley biography had not intervened, it is doubtful that Dowden would have finished such a study on Goethe as he had planned, because he had become increasingly convinced that his best work in criticism was to be done about authors of his own language. Nevertheless, Goethe never lost his attraction for Dowden, who considered him to be the greatest poet of the last three centuries and aimed to resume his study of him after completing his *Shelley.* The nature of Goethe's attraction for Dowden and the similarity of their viewpoints are most succinctly expressed in Dowden's interpretation of *Faust:* "And Goethe (ever toiling with magnificent will) makes the whole of Faust the celebration of Divine grace. The poem is surrounded by the Divine presence in the universe; Faust is from first to last under the care of God. But Grace is not concentrated in magic emblems and charms and relics, it spreads wide and free over the whole universe. It resides in Nature (part 2, sc. 1st). It is lodged in persons—it cooperates with every effort of man towards growth—it acts when he cannot act himself." [16] In later years, during a summer's vacation, Dowden translated Goethe's "East Western Divan" into English verse, and he also published five essays on Goethe in *New Studies in Literature* (1895). For twenty-three years he was president of the Goethe Society, but he declined membership in the Shelley Society.

Dowden worked steadily on the *Life of Shelley* from 1883 until its publication in the late fall of 1886 in two beautifully bound volumes. Since a great number of people who possessed Shelley-ana had offered him their resources, he had had access to manuscripts and fresh information not previously available. Dowden was, for example, the first biographer of Shelley to have free access to all the Shelley papers preserved by Sir Percy and Lady Shelley, including the journals of Mary Shelley and her correspondence with Shelley. From the Reverend C. E. Esdaile, the poet's grandson, the child of his daughter Ianthe, Dowden obtained a volume of manuscript poetry, half of the poems unpublished and previously unknown. He had free access as well to the Shelley materials possessed by William Rossetti, as mentioned previously, and by Dr. Richard Garnett of the British Museum. After two years of correspondence and promised payment, Dowden obtained the use of Shelley materials owned by H. Buxtom Forman, including Claire Clairmont's journals.[17] He had the advantage also—if not disadvantage—of the previous attempts at writing Shelley's biography as a whole or in part by Thomas Jefferson Hogg, Leigh Hunt, John Cordy Jeaffreson, Thomas Medwin, Thomas Lane Peacock, William Rossetti, Lady Shelley, John Addington Symonds, and Edward John Trelawney, as well as of numerous journal articles about Shelley's life.

Dowden aimed to write an authoritative record of the poet that would last, to present the facts about him as he found them, and to be as exhaustive and accurate as possible. And he presented quite justly the strengths and weaknesses of Shelley's nature—the beauty of his ideals as well as the grisly conduct intertwined with it. Dowden endeavored to understand Shelley, which was more difficult than to exalt or to degrade him.

Not a critical biography, Dowden's *Shelley* is chiefly narrative and descriptive. There is little analysis and no explication of Shelley's poetry; the *Life* is concerned rather with the growth and development of Shelley's mind from boyhood to young adulthood as revealed in his life and works. In the minutest detail, Dowden presents Shelley as an inveterate idealist, one too far removed from the prosaic facts of actual life to be practical. Dowden traces Shelley's quarrel with the world, his rejection of all institutions and traditions of the past and present, and his projection of an idyllic future state of society when men shall govern themselves by love. But Dowden also presents Shelley as betrayed by his ideals into weakness and error; for the ideal future, imagined so intensely by Shelley, could never be realized, Dowden would have one believe; therefore, it ought not to have been desired. Such a projection of the perfection of man is based on the misconception that evil resides in external powers rather than in man's heart and will. Although such illusions may be of service in keeping alive within men an aspiration for the highest things, they assuredly have a dangerous tendency to draw men away from ordinary reality and to take from them some of the fountains of genuine feeling which are needed to freshen and brighten everyday experience.

It follows, of course, that Dowden adopted a specific vantage point from which to view Shelley; as a result, though the presentation of facts and documents is free from partisanship and moralizing, the interpretation of the facts is typically Dowden's. Dowden requires a poet with his head in a cloud of ideals, such as Shelley, to keep realistically in touch with the empirical facts of existence. Shelley failed the test. Shelley, instead of restraining himself by facts and life, sought stability in abstract theory rather than in concrete fact. Had he lived longer, Dowden affirms, his "wild ideals" would gradually have been succeeded by wiser principles —ones more realistically rooted in things as they are.

A number of new points about Shelley's life and works appeared in the biography. For the first time, the biographical nature of Mary Shelley's novel, *Lodore*, published in 1835, is pointed out; for Dowden makes clear that the events and characters of *Lodore* bear a striking resemblance to Shelley's life.[18] New information concerning Shelley's life at Eton also is added through the generosity of various informants. And fresh facts relating to the residence of Shelley and his bride, Harriet Westbrook, in Edinburgh, Keswick, Dublin, London, and Wales are included.[19] Also new to Shelley biography is the inclusion of Shelley's report of the incident of Thomas Jefferson Hogg's attempt to seduce his first wife, Harriet. Precise facts of the Chancery Court proceedings to obtain custody of his and Harriet's children which appear here were never told before. New also is the information of Claire Clairmont's letter to Lord Byron, written to say that Mary Shelley knew nothing of Byron's and her intimacy and to instruct Byron to address her under an assumed name if he wished to communicate. The information here presented from the correspondence between William Godwin and Shelley sheds new light on both personalities: Shelley, as generous to a fault; Godwin, as inconsistent and inconsiderate.

The most significant new feature in the biography concerned Harriet, against whom Dowden insinuated charges of immorality after her separation from Shelley; and he cited Shelley's suspicions of her unfaithfulness to him before the separation. Dowden attempted to show that Harriet's defection was the logical outcome of the teaching of Godwin and Shelley, for Godwin taught that a marriage ceased to exist when it was no longer rooted in love. The *Quarterly Review* (April, 1887) severely reprehended Dowden's defamation of Harriet as an "unjustifiable breach of the golden rule of advocacy." Accusing Dowden of vindicating Shelley by casting shame on Harriet, the *Review* facetiously suggested the cause to be the difficult position occupied by Dowden in being obligated to Shelley's surviving relatives. His charges of immorality, it claimed, are "unverified and unverifiable." Furthermore, to have made a charge which could not be proved was "unworthy of Professor Dowden's reputation." Dowden defended himself immediately in a counterreply in the *Athenaeum* (1887);

The reviewer speaks of me as having yielded to influence coming from Shelley's surviving relatives, and in consequence, of having insinuated charges of immorality against Harriet Shelley. I wonder a little at the confidence with which the reviewer makes an assertion on a matter about which he knows nothing. The only document temporarily withheld from my use by Sir Percy and Lady Shelley was the one and only document in their possession which reflects on Harriet Shelley's conduct previous to the separation from Shelley. Evidence was collected by me from various quarters, and I decided that all the facts must be told to my readers. On me, therefore, rests the full and sole responsibility for setting forth those facts. I do not contend that Harriet actually broke her marriage vow before the separation. I give my reader grounds for believing that Shelley thought that she was untrue to him; and I express my own opinion that Shelley in this instance, as in many others, may have erred in judgment. It must be borne in mind, as explaining in some degree, Shelley's subsequent relations with Harriet, that if he were sincerely a believer in Godwin's revolutionary principles, respecting marriage, he could not look on such unfaithfulness as a *crime*, though it would be the last and complete proof that his wife had ceased to love him. Having ceased to love him, according to the principles professed by Shelley, she was free to enter into a new union with another and so was he; and each might still remain the friend of the other.

The facetious charge of the *Quarterly Review* that Dowden was straddling a difficult problem may have had more than a shade of truth in it because he was tempted to discontinue his biography as a result of the Shelley diplomacies: Harriet Shelley's grandchildren were unwilling to release any materials which might soil her reputation, and Sir Percy and Lady Shelley thought Dowden too much the champion of Harriet's cause. Dowden wrote in his diary on September 23, 1883, that Lady Shelley's theory was that both Hogg and Peacock made love to Harriet after her marriage. Whether or not they were repulsed, Lady Shelley could not know.

What caused the misunderstanding and, therefore, Dowden's reprehension by the *Quarterly Review* was that Dowden had not made enough of his important discovery of a letter addressed by Shelley to Harriet in which he had stated that he had given up all hopes of a true marriage with her but preferred nonetheless to remain with her. Harriet, however, rejected his advances for a reconciliation; consequently, she drove him from her, or so wrote Dr. Garnett to Dowden in a judicious appraisal of the information of the letter.[20] Dowden's defense in the *Athenaeum* attempted belatedly to emphasize the importance of this discovery. But, even if he had greatly emphasized his discovery earlier, there was so much contrary evidence in favor of Harriet's innocence that the question would have remained an open one. As stated in 1940 by Newman Ivey White: "No biographer since Dowden credited the idea. . . . But Professor Dowden used the story of infidelity, not to endorse it, but to show that Shelley's belief in it justified Shelley's conduct to himself." [21]

On the whole, the *Life* was favorably received. To the reviewer in the *Spectator*, this *Life of Shelley* superseded all others since it both sifted and appraised the valuable materials previously accumulated for a life of Shelley; the *Graphic* applauded the biography as a definitive edition; and the *Critic* judged it as good a biography as Boswell's *Johnson* and Moore's *Byron*. The biography subsequently became established as the definitive life of Shelley and went through seven reprintings, the latest in 1951. It was superseded only by Newman Ivey White's biography of the poet, published in 1940. A summary of the *Life* appeared as an introduction to a single-volume edition of Shelley's poetry, edited later by Dowden. The chief contribution of this volume to similar editions of Shelley's poetry already in existence is this fine eighteen-page introduction.

Besides Dowden's work on Shelley and his occasional trips to England to consult with the Shelleys and various other informants and beside his regular lectures in the classroom at Trinity, Dowden was occupied with the contribution of articles and reviews and with meetings of the National Library Committee, the Historical Society, the Philosophical Society, the Goethe Society, the Shakespeare Society, the Wordsworth Society, the Royal Society of Dublin, and the Browning Society, which he was asked to chair. "Endless committees cut up my time," he sighed; "and I wish I could be clothed like the lilies by looking up at the sky, instead of attending meetings." [22] And, since he was always remembered as a specialist on Shakespeare, he also received numerous invitations to lecture or to write about the great Elizabethan. He wrote introductions to the *International Shakespeare* and to Irving and Marshall's edition of Shakespeare's works. He published a lithographed facsimile of *The Passionate Pilgrim* (1599), reputedly by William Shakespeare, Christopher Marlowe, Richard Barnfield, Bartholomew Griffin, and other, unknown writers. *The Passionate Pilgrim* is a slender volume made up of pieces of verse, many of which are certainly not by Shakespeare, although his name appears on the title page.

In the spring of 1883 Dowden was a candidate for the Clark Lectureship in English Literature at Trinity College, Cambridge. Among the most distinguished writers of recommendations for him were Matthew Arnold, Hallam Tennyson, D. G. Rossetti, J. C. Shairp, F. J. Furnivall, Stopford Brooke, David Masson, and Sir Henry Taylor. Dowden, however, was not elected; Leslie Stephen, his friend, was chosen instead. After being elected, Stephen wrote a friendly note to Dowden, stating that his one advantage over Dowden was his seniority. Later, however, Dowden was offered the Clark Lectureship at Cambridge for 1893–96, which consisted of twelve lectures.

In October, 1884, Dowden received an invitation from Daniel Coit Gilman, the president of the Johns Hopkins University in Baltimore, Maryland. The university offered him a chair if he would start an English literature department and deliver annually forty-two lectures at a salary of one thousand pounds, four hundred more than his salary at Trinity College. If he could not accept this offer, he was invited to give at least a series of lectures. Dowden's work on Shelley and his deep roots in Ireland imposed obligations, however, which he felt could not be met abroad; and therefore he decided to remain in Dublin. Another invitation to lecture came in the summer of 1890 from the Chautauqua University in America; but, when he finally visited America in 1896, he went to Princeton University to lecture.

VII *Editions and More Essays*

Even while writing Shelley, Dowden was contemplating an edition of Wordsworth's poetry. Aubrey de Vere, who had been personally acquainted with Wordsworth and who was enthusiastic about his poetry, had been encouraging Dowden for a number of years to write a volume of criticism about Wordsworth that would be comparable to his Shakespeare study. A disparaging criticism of a current work about Wordsworth had stirred de Vere to prod Dowden harder for a critical study that would establish the great Romantic poet in the honored place he deserved. And, when Dowden finished the biography of Shelley in 1886, de Vere again urged the study of Wordsworth. To this end he had sent Dowden his own notes about the life and mind of Wordsworth. Dowden, an early disciple, always a great admirer of Wordsworth, and an active member of the Wordsworth Society, was not uninterested in de Vere's suggestion. He had already contributed at least three articles on Wordsworth by 1883, in spite of his many other commitments,[23] as well as his Introduction to *The Prose Works of William Wordsworth*, edited by A. B. Grosart in 1875. But not until the 1890s was he able to find time to begin a systematic study of Wordsworth's life and works.

The first of Dowden's volumes on Wordsworth finally appeared in the late spring of 1890—an edition of Wordsworth's *Lyrical Ballads, 1798*. In an excellent preface Dowden presented something of the history of the volume and indicated its significance in English literature. For the next two years most of his time was spent in editing Wordsworth's poetry, a work published subsequently in seven volumes, *The Poetical Works of William Wordsworth* (1892). Dowden followed Wordsworth's own arrangement of the poems in the last text of his life, 1849–50. The most important variations of the text and everything worth knowing about the occasion and evolution of each poem appear at the end of each volume. A single-volume edition, a selection of Wordsworth's poems, appeared later, *Poems of William Wordsworth: A Selection* (1897).

Dowden's friend, Aubrey de Vere, who had been prodding him to produce such work, should have been content with one or another of these works; and, to an extent, he was. But, as much will have more, he suggested that Dowden prepare a companion volume, containing Colerdige's best poems and a three-volume edition of Southey's poetry. The latter was undertaken, and *Poems by Southey* was edited and published in 1895. A volume on Coleridge, however, never appeared, though an article on Coleridge as a poet did appear in 1896 in the *Saturday Review*.

A decline in health early in 1887 prohibited Dowden from carrying on his work for several months, but by April he was slowly advancing with several projects. He had been invited by Macmillan in 1885 to write a fourth volume of a *History of English Literature* (1780 onwards); and Stopford Brooke, Edmund Gosse, and George Saintsbury were to prepare the earlier volumes. In Dowden's characteristic critical-historical approach, he planned to give the usual little biographical sketch of each author and the critical remarks about his works in chronological order, and he hoped the book would be suitable for classroom teaching. Because of fundamental disagreement with Saintsbury's critical approach to literature, however, which Dowden expected to be continued by Gosse, he debated with himself two years later about continuing the project. Dowden was persuaded, however, by Macmillan that his fears were unfounded since Stopford Brooke at least would agree with Dowden's view.

Despite the publisher's assurances, the difference in critical ap-

proaches seemingly deepened because Dowden's contribution to
the *History* was not published, nor is a manuscript of it extant; yet
the greater part of his manuscript was in Gosse's hands by February, 1897, and Dowden counted on its publication by June. In a
letter from Garnett to Dowden in August, 1900, there is a hint
that the differences may have become irreconcilable since Dowden proposed a competitive history of English literature with
Garnett as a possible editor; however, Garnett politely but firmly
rejected this proposal. Evidently, Dowden withdrew his manuscript from the Macmillan project; and, whatever the material he
had prepared, it presumably appeared in new arrangement as
New Studies in Literature (1895).

In 1887 Dowden was also reading through the great mass of Sir
Henry Taylor's correspondence to prepare his letters for publication. *The Correspondence of Henry Taylor,* published in 1888,
was intended as a companion volume to Taylor's autobiography.
Sir Henry himself had gone through his letters a few years before
his death to cancel passages unsuitable for publication; hence,
nothing appears in Dowden's volume which did not have Sir
Henry's sanction. The letters relate a variety of interests—literature, state affairs, society, wisdom, and social grace. Dowden admired Sir Henry more as a poet than as a letter writer, however,
because his poetry was based on observable facts and affairs. To
Dowden, Sir Henry was the first poet since Milton to keep the
poetic imagination in touch with the life of affairs. Without doubt
that energetic Irish gadfly Aubrey de Vere was also the stimulator
of this edition of letters, for de Vere had been very intimate with
Sir Henry, had traveled with him on the Continent, and had
thought him the greatest dramatic poet since Shakespeare.

Dowden also published in 1888 his *Transcripts and Studies,* a
second anthology of essays; and he included in it two transcripts
as well. He published for the first time transcripts of Shelley's
"Philosophical View of Reform" and of Carlyle's lectures, "On the
Periods of European Culture." Dowden had discovered Shelley's
essay among the materials owned by Sir Percy and Lady Shelley
while writing the *Life of Shelley* but to have introduced a full
account of this unpublished work in his *Life* would have interrupted the narrative with a digression of unsuitable length. Yet,
because of the significant relationship of the subject of the essay
to Shelley's mature thought and feelings, or even as a prose com-

mentary on his later poems, Dowden realized the need to publish it. The transcript of Carlyle's lectures was derived from a manuscript of over two hundred and fifty pages which Dowden had discovered. A shorthand report, ten of the eleven lectures (only one, the ninth, was missing) were fully recorded by Dowden. Critical studies on Shelley, Spenser, Marlowe, Shakespeare, Browning, Wordsworth, and Victorian literature were the heart of the volume. Perhaps the two most significant of these essays are "Last Words on Shelley," a defense and a final reply to the criticism of his *Life of Shelley,* and "The Interpretation of Literature," a concise statement about the function of the poet and of literary criticism.

In "Last Words on Shelley" Dowden defines three kinds of men in life and literature: the craftsman, the conqueror, and the lover. The craftsmen "put true and exact work into all they offer to the world, and find their happiness in such faithful service." The conquerors are the masters of life; the most eminent representatives are Shakespeare and Goethe: "It is their part to bring into actual union, as far as our mortal life permits, what is real and what is ideal." The lovers live in the ideal alone; like Shelley, they are "men who can never quite reconcile the two worlds in which we have our being, the world of material fact and the spiritual world above and beyond it; who give themselves away for love or give themselves away for light." It would have been more to the point had Dowden called the craftsmen "realists" who live for the material alone; the conquerors, "realist-idealists" who attempt to fuse the material and the ideal or spiritual; and the lovers, "idealists" who live for the ideal alone. The expression of his literary theory differs in no substantial way from that expressed in his earlier publication on literary criticism.

VIII   *Relation to the Yeatses and Irish Literature*

During the 1880s Dowden began to recognize W. B. Yeats's talents. "An interesting bow of hope in the clouds," Dowden described him: "He hangs in the balance between genius and (to speak rudely) fool. I shall rejoice in the first." [24] The social interchange between the Yeatses and Dowden, which had begun in the 1860s, lasted for many years. Dowden entertained W. B. Yeats and his father at occasional breakfasts in his home, and he lent books from his library to the young Yeats. Ironically, in the home

of the professor who would not touch "the Theosophy Movement
with a long pole" (as H. O. White stated), it was because of a
discussion of A. P. Sinnett's *Esoteric Buddhism* and *The Occult
World* that Yeats, Charles Johnston, and George Russell became
interested in Eastern mythologies. They founded a branch of the
Theosophical Society, which, according to John Eglinton, "was as
truly the nucleus from which the Irish Literary Renaissance origi-
nated as were the contemporary Gaelic and literary societies."[25]

Private mythologies of any kind, ones not rooted in the universal experience of mankind, appeared to Dowden to be an escape
from the pressure of facts; and this deeply rooted conviction
against the esoteric and provincial precluded Dowden's participation in the revival of Celtic literature to which Yeats and George
Russell were to contribute greatly. Dowden had been sitting for
his portrait by the elder Yeats, who had a studio in Dublin at the
time; and, during this time, to ensure payment for an edition of
Mosada, a Moorish story by the young Yeats which Dowden
liked, he assisted the poet's father in collecting a few subscribers.
W. B. Yeats's father and Dowden also used to ramble together
over the Dublin countryside, especially along the scenic footpaths
by the Irish Sea near Howth to read poetry, to criticize painting,
and to argue about esthetics. Privately, Dowden encouraged the
young Yeats; and, after the publication of *The Wanderings of
Oisin and Other Poems,* he wrote a note of warm congratulations;
but Dowden never publicly encouraged the aspiring young poet.
In fact, Dowden never published any critical articles about Yeats,
although he lived to see the publications of Yeats's more mature
pieces such as *The Trembling of the Veil* and *The Countess Kath-
leen and Various Legends and Lyrics.*

Nor was Yeats the only Irish writer Dowden ignored. Dowden's
close friends, Samuel Ferguson, Aubrey de Vere, and John Todhunter—all contributors to the newly revived Celtic literature—
were strangely missing from his critical evaluations. For a reason
which his friends could not understand, Dowden isolated himself
completely from the Irish movement. And the irony of his isolation, to them, was that he not only knew their works but had
commended them privately. A letter concerning Dr. Todhunter
evinces Dowden's awareness of the effect of his aloofness from the
literature of his friends. Somewhat apologetically he wrote to his
friend, Elizabeth Dickinson West, on her removal to Bedford

Park: ". . . now with your brother H. you will be near Dr. Tod-hunter. . . . I fear that he thinks I have turned indifferent to him, and grown narrow and tame, but I think of him with great regard." [26] Unable to resist the attractions of Irish subjects, Dr. Todhunter had contributed to *Poems and Ballads of Young Ire-land* and had published *The Banshee and Other Poems* with a dedicatory acknowledgement of his inspiration from Standish O'Grady, an early senior enthusiast for Irish literature, who was regarded by every important Irish revivalist as "father of us all."

In the late 1880s until his death, Dowden lectured at various patriotic meetings in favor of maintaining the political alliance of Ireland with England, attended Unionist demonstrations, assisted as secretary of the Liberal Union, founded a Unionist Club, worked "for some months on nothing but Unionist work" in the Irish office, led the Irish Unionist Alliance, and even requested from Swinburne a Unionist song. Dowden became a Unionist not because he believed that the union had brought peace or prosper-ity to Ireland, but because he firmly believed that the Separatist party too little regarded the wholeness of things—it cut itself off too hastily from hereditary influence and operated apart from the total complexity of structured government. Dowden also had a deep respect for order as being inherent in the elemental nature of man and things: "The plunder, the midnight outrages, the card-ings, the maiming, the torturing of dumb animals, the slaying of men and women during the days when the law of the League [the Nationalists] governed the land" [27] denied such order. To Dow-den, civil liberty was vainly sought by those who he believed did not possess human liberty—a liberty which best expresses itself in the man who attends to the duty that is nearest him and who seeks to enlarge the sphere of his beneficent activity, a liberty which evidences itself in the tough moral fiber of a people. In the moral quality of a people "must the ultimate salvation be sought for." [28] To Dowden, moral characteristics were identical to an ac-knowledgment of the *universal* nature of truth and to a respect, therefore, for the contributions of others both in the present and in the past who are and were concerned with truth. To him Ire-land was divided between those who recognized the existence of such order and those who did not. And, because of this conviction, Dowden took considerable interest in the maintenance of the Union.

In 1889, Dowden presented the first of the annual Taylorian lectures at Oxford University. Among the ten other scholars selected to give the lectures were Walter Pater and William Rossetti. Dealing with some subject of foreign literature, the lectures were to encourage the study of foreign letters in, as well as beyond, the university. The lectures were subsequently published in 1900 as *Studies in European Literature*. Dowden's lecture, "Literary Criticism in France" is a study of Sainte-Beuve, Edmond Scherer, Désiré Nisard, Ferdinand Brunetière, and Hippolyte Adolphe Taine, all of whom he had also discussed in his *New Studies in Literature* (1895). The central fact of the lecture was its demonstration of the turning of literature and literary criticism from the subjective, lyrical, and personal to an intensive study of the external world and of the life of man in society.

Suddenly and unexpectedly in October, 1892, Dowden's wife died after an unsuccessful operation, one year after their silver wedding anniversary. Since she had been quite well before her final illness, her death was a terrible blow, and it affected Dowden considerably. Hester, the oldest daughter, returned home from her piano studies in London to take charge of home duties; for her father was almost inconsolable from grief and was broken by depression. Hester married four years later Dr. Travers-Smith, a prominent physician in Dublin. Richard, the only son, became a physician, married in 1900, and obtained a post in Jamaica. Only Hilda remained at home for any length of time.

Invited in 1893 by Cambridge University to become Clark Lecturer, a position of visiting professor which continued for three years, Dowden presented a series of studies on the French Revolution and English literature.

But little work was done and little published by Dowden for a few years after his wife's death. In 1895 Dowden married Elizabeth Dickinson West; and though he needed no longer to write to supplement his salary, he once more produced vigorously. He published an edition of *Poems of Robert Southey* (1895) and another anthology of his collected essays, *New Studies in Literature* (1895). Southey's poetry, wrote Dowden, acquires its significance to the reader not because of its great original thought or feeling, nor because of its flawless lyrical qualities, but because of its celebration of a universal moral order and of worthy heroic action.

New Studies in Literature contains thirteen essays which are chiefly descriptive studies of the life and works of eighteenth- and nineteenth-century authors; and these essays were selected from a larger group which had previously appeared in *The Fortnightly Review*. The Introduction, the most significant essay in the anthology, is surely Dowden's answer to a growing concern among his friends as to his lack of participation in the Irish Renaissance:

In Ireland at present, apart from the Universities—we must sorrowfully acknowledge the fact—little interest is taken in literature; but we can conceive an Irish literary movement which should command our deepest interest and sympathy; a movement in which such differences of national character as may perhaps exist should manifest themselves not of deliberate purpose, but naturally and spontaneously. But if the Irish literary movement were to consist in flapping a green banner in the eyes of the beholders, and upthrusting a pasteboard "sunburst" high in the air, I for one, should prefer to stand quietly apart from such a movement. . . . No folly can be geater than that of fancying that we shall strengthen our literary position by living exclusively in our own ideas, and showing ourselves inhospitable to the best ideas of other lands.

IX *Visit to America*

Dowden twice crossed the Atlantic: in 1896, he lectured at Princeton University on the occasion of its sesquicentennial and received there his fourth honorary doctoral degree; in 1911, he visited Quebec in an effort to overcome increasing insomnia and to recover from failing health. In Princeton, he gave six lectures about the French Revolution and its relationship to English literature; and, among the friends he made while there was Professor Woodrow Wilson, later President of the United States. In 1897, Dowden's lectures, which were essentially revisions of those presented by him as Clark Lecturer at Cambridge University, were published as *The French Revolution and English Literature*. The lectures repeat in essence, but in much greater detail, the ideas expressed in embryo in his essay, "The French Revolution and Literature," which had been published in *Studies in Literature* (1887).

During this year Dowden also published *A History of French Literature* in the series of "Short Histories of the World," edited by Edmund Gosse. This book is surprisingly monotonous and mediocre in style and content when compared with his other works, for only rarely does the text flash with the inspiration and vivacity of his own critical insight, and then it does so with writers whose works show some kind of moral energy. A curious omission is Charles Baudelaire, who, belonging to the age of Victor Hugo, Théophile Gautier, and the Romanticists, should have been included with them. Without doubt, Dowden's work suffers from having been too hastily written and from relying too heavily on its French sources, especially on Petit de Julleville's *Histoire,* which is far more interesting than Dowden's. Indeed, Dowden's *History* is in essence a précis of the Frenchman's, and it has value only as a guidebook for beginners.

During his visit to America, Dowden caught a cold that stubbornly resisted treatment, and he suffered increasingly during the succeeding winters from chronic bronchitis. His health declined so much that in 1899 he considered either getting an assistant-lecturer or resigning his position completely. In 1910, when his health was failing again, W. B. Yeats was suggested as his successor. When Yeats, not wishing to conceal his physical limitations because of his poor eyes, told Professor Mahaffy of Trinity that he would need to be read to, Dowden suggested that Yeats be excused from teaching early English literature which would require his having to read a great deal. But Dowden's health improved—as did, coincidentally, Yeats's eyes. When Dowden died three years later, Professor William Trench, described by Yeats as "a man of known sobriety of manner and of mind," was appointed to the chair vacated by Dowden.

By Christmas Day, 1900, Dowden was sending copies of *Puritan and Anglican,* his most recent book, to his friends. An anthology of revised lectures, this work concentrated on seventeenth-century writers: Sir Thomas Browne, Richard Hooker, Herbert Vaughan, John Milton, Jeremy Taylor, Richard Baxter, John Bunyan, and Samuel Butler. As a guide to the theological trends of the seventeenth century, Dowden used his brother's book on the history of the church, but he dealt chiefly with the imaginative aspects of the writings of these authors. The words *Puritan* and *Anglican* adopt new significance in the study: as well as referring to certain communities of Christian faith, they denote two types of mind: the Catholic and the Puritan, "to one of which the visible and the invisible are only different aspects of one great reality, while to the other they stand apart as sundered or even as antagonistic powers." [29] To the Catholic type of mind, "external apparatus" becomes avenues and inlets for the Divine influence; to the Puritan, on the other hand, external phenomena become barriers that inhibit the soul's apprehension of the Divine.

A curious explanation of the basis of selection of authors also attracts attention in the Introduction: ". . . among such writers I have spoken only of those who move me to speak through some personal interest which I feel in the men or their work." Analysis of what is said about each writer reveals certain ideals common both to the author studied and to Dowden—a respect, even awe and wonder, for nature; a regard for circumstances past, present, and future in formulating principles; a recognition of divinity in man and in nature; and an acknowledgment of the place and validity of reason in the pursuit of truth.

In the next few years Dowden worked on biographies of Robert Browning and Montaigne. During the latter half of 1902, he worked steadily on the research for a Browning biography to be included in "The Temple Biographies" series. Published in February, 1904, this biography went through two editions during the year. It was the first biographical-critical life of Browning to be published, though Dowden tends to expound upon the poems rather than to analyze them. Written after a pattern much like that of *Shakspere: A Critical Study of His Mind and Art,* the book considers the life and works of Browning chronologically, drawing no sharp line between the biographical and critical aspects.

Dowden presents Browning as a militant Transcendentalist, who, in inheriting the Transcendentalism of his predecessors and in absorbing the scientific spirit of his contemporaries, attempted to save the truths of Transcendentalism from the skeptical intellects of his time. Browning, gifted with a mystical imagination and with an athletic intellect, set out to defend mystical apprehension of reality, the truths of the heart. Man's impulses towards knowledge, beauty, and love were reverenced by Browning as the natural signs of the existence of a world extending beyond that of the senses.

When the American editor Alexander Jessup asked Dowden to write about some French author for a "French Men of Letters" series for Lippincott Press, which aimed to do for French literature what the "English Men of Letters" series did for English literature, Dowden suggested that he write on Montaigne. Dowden's *Montaigne,* published in 1905, was the first volume of the biographical and critical series. There was not much that was original to be said about Montaigne, for many books about the Frenchman were already available; indeed, Dowden drew the material for his study from ninety-nine books by and about the Frenchman from his own bookshelves, a collection which included those of chief importance in Montaigne studies. He made his study a better introduction, or handbook, to Montaigne's essays than had yet appeared; and he did so by using the writer's own words from the essays to illustrate, as much as possible, some particular aspect of his life and development.

The central result of all Montaigne's thought, Dowden informs us, is: "It is an absolute perfection, and as it were divine, for a man to know how to enjoy loyally his being. A doctrine of hedonism, certainly, but as Montaigne understood it, it embraced the whole art of living completely and living aright. He was a humanist, but he was also a moralist who taught that the pursuit of virtue is in itself a joy. He would not allow that body and soul should be regarded apart. There is in us nothing that is purely corporeal or purely ethereal." Dowden wrote the book with pleasure, for he had found much to admire in Montaigne.

When a publisher offered to reprint Dowden's poems with some new additions in 1908, Dowden had no desire to reemerge as a poet. However, a slender volume, *A Woman's Reliquary,* containing a sequence of one hundred love lyrics written since the early collection of poetry, was published posthumously in 1913. These songs, presumably addressed to his second wife throughout the years of their friendship and marriage, are much more spontaneous and melodious than those in his first book. Most of them are experiments with iambic tetrameter in quatrains (two in each poem). The sequence moves thematically from Dowden's early acquaintance with Elizabeth Dickinson West to their marriage in their late years. Tenderness and gentle passion, deep respect and patient love, sparkling and quiet joy reign as the spirit of the poems, as of their long friendship. Perhaps only George Meredith's and Elizabeth Barrett Browning's poems surpass in statement the exhilarating satisfaction of companionship that is expressed in these lyrics.

Much of Dowden's time after 1908 was spent in rest and recreation, for even the necessity of standing to lecture was becoming increasingly more difficult. The sea trip to Quebec for two weeks in 1911, taken as a health restorative, did not improve his condition. His final book appeared in 1910, *Essays Modern and Elizabethan*, which consisted of lectures reprinted from previously published articles. Only five of the fourteen are Elizabethan, and the more significant are not among them, though Dowden is to be commended for attempting to extend sound knowledge of Elizabethan poetry and prose as Coleridge and Hazlitt had conceived it. Several essays are based on unpublished manuscripts in his possession. The most interesting are two manuscripts about William Cowper, written in 1794 and 1809, which give the details of the friendly conspiracy by which William Hayley and Lady Hesketh hoped to lift the cloud of depression from Cowper. By far the best essays are on more recent authors—Walter Pater, Henrik Ibsen, Heinrich Heine, and Goethe.

Especially significant in the Pater essay is Dowden's rejection of the commonly accepted interpretation which represents Marius's experience in the house of Cecilia as only an extension of a refined hedonism so as to include within it new pleasures of the moral sense or the religious temper. To Dowden, Marius's aim had never been pleasure but perfection, of which he now discovered that he had an inadequate perception that needed to be corrected by freshly gained insights. Dowden also sees in Pater proofs supporting his own philosophy of existence. In his essays on Ibsen, Heine, and Goethe, he emphasizes similarly those aspects of their life-experience which correspond in some way to his own. Ibsen, like Dowden, conceives a complete human personality as constituted by intellect apprehending a truth, by love expounding its significance, and by will incarnating it in action. Heine, like Dowden, discovers all things partaking of divinity. And Goethe, also like Dowden, believes knowledge to be gained by the harmonious compenetration of head and heart. As Dowden stated of Taine, so now may one judge his work in these essays: "The works of this writer or of that are studied not for their own sakes, but in order that they may furnish proofs of the thesis of the . . . critic." [30]

During 1913, the year that was his last, Dowden prepared a series of wholly new lectures in which he traced the protest

52   EDWARD DOWDEN

against nineteenth-century materialism from Wordsworth and Southey to Ruskin's sociological ideas and to William Morris's Socialism. The volume in which he hoped to publish these never materialized, for he died of a heart attack on April 3, 1913.

CHAPTER 2

Via Media: World-View

> I am quite aware that many persons
> say my position is an untenable *via
> media*—but I retort that it is not
> —*Fragments from Old Letters,* I, p.
> 166.

I *Intellectual Milieu and Philosophical Background*

AS a representative of the conscience of his times, Dowden reflects the soul-shaking struggles and conflicting loyalties that characterized the Victorian era, through the greater part of which he lived. On the religious level, biblical criticism, introduced from the Continent by the works of David Friedrich Strauss and Joseph Ernest Renan, challenged the complacently comfortable Anglican Church, which was embedded in a dogma no longer believed tenable. On the philosophical level, the Copernican revolution in the philosophy of the preceding century, effected by Immanuel Kant's *Critiques,* shattered man's hopes of attaining true objective knowledge. On the social level, the old order of a patriarchal government by aristocrats was giving way to a representational one by plebiscite. On the scientific and industrial scene, rapid progress in technological innovations transformed England from an agricultural to an industrial nation within less than one generation. The biological scientists' postulate of a theory of evolution inspired in such writers as Herbert Spencer a belief in the progress of mankind towards ultimate perfection: man might once have been an ape, but he could some day be an angel.

In brief, the shift in religious, philosophical, social, and economic beliefs during the nineteenth century provoked a restlessness of spirit, disquieted the once orthodox intellect with religious and philosophical doubts, removed familiar old landmarks in economics and politics, and substituted new optimistic and political freedoms. Indeed, few individuals could sing with heartfelt conviction both clauses in the exultant lyric of Pippa—"God's in His heaven—All's right with the world!" One of those influenced to the marrow of his spirit by *la maladie du siècle* was Dowden, for no aspect of his viewpoint remained untouched by the fluctuating intellectual currents of his times.

The nineteenth century saw at its beginning the official demise of the neo-Classical principles of art with the publication of the second edition of Wordsworth's *Lyrical Ballads* (1800). The Preface to this edition came to be known as the literary manifesto of Romantic freedom. In the Preface, Wordsworth worked into a critical theory what had been increasingly accepted and practiced by the close of the eighteenth century: he authoritatively reported the end of the tyranny of rules which attempted to control eighteenth-century taste, and he sanctioned the individual feelings common to all men as providing the new standard for art. He declared that "all good poetry is the spontaneous overflow of powerful feelings," and this declaration gave Romanticism its official initiation and theoretical defense.

The neo-Classicists of the eighteenth century had sought for general rather than individual truths; they had subordinated imagination to reason; and they had preferred restraint, decorum, and simplicity of expression to exuberance, passion, and spontaneity. To them, as Dowden succinctly summarized the spirit of much of the thought of the eighteenth century, "Truth was now to be pursued, if at all, not by any winged flight into the empyrean, but by careful treading of the substantial earth. The passions were to be retracted within the bounds of what is reasonable. To ascertain facts, to observe phenomena, to analyze combinations of things, seemed better than to manipulate mysterious words or to start from magnificent assumptions." [1] The product of this creed was belief in the rationally attested Deity of the Deists who was the Watchmaker who set in motion the observable mechanics of the universe; in human minds as passive in the perception of facts, as active only in the analysis and comparison of phenomena; and in a dead, mechanical world of nature, the essence of which man could never know.

Wordsworth's theoretical manifesto of literary freedom, which was adopted and developed by the Romantics, went counter to the emphasis of the eighteenth century and focused attention not on external phenomena but on the nature within us. Freedom in life and literature was to be attained, therefore, by recognizing the truth brought by way of the passions of man. Philosophical support on which the Romantics could rest their claims to faith in the intuitive passions as reliable purveyors of truth was provided by Immanuel Kant in whose rationalism the eighteenth century found its own destroyer, for Kant's *Critique of Pure Reason* (1781) undercut the rationalistic support of philosophy and theology. Metaphysics, he argued, must be ruled out as not constituting real knowledge: all discourse about ultimates, universals, and supernaturals had to be eliminated because such abstracts transcend experience. Since *pure* reason could entertain only empirical knowledge—only those things which address themselves to man spatially or temporally—man could talk only about the phenomena he senses. But such *a posteriori* knowledge is modified by frames of time, space, unity, and causality which are not empirical: the mind conditions *a posteriori* knowledge by *a priori* frames, for the eye confers as well as receives. On the basis of this fact Kant proceeded to argue for the validity of *practical* reason: the means by which the mind envisions things, such as the supernatural, that it cannot incorporate into empirical knowledge.

For hundreds of years theology had used philosophic concepts in support of its claims, but theology could now no longer depend on philosophy. Instead, Kant (a good Lutheran!) reasserted the truth-claims of religion in terms closely allied with man's ethical concerns. Reason is capable, he contended, of making ethical judgment beyond the actuality; it is compelled by a moral "oughtness," by a moral law which calls man to a new beginning. But, since the realization of moral demands is not possible in this life, it must take place in the one after death. Hence, he continued, the very nature of the moral law demands the postulate of immortality. Kant, recognizing that he had, with the doctrine of pure reason, dismissed the supernatural, then used his doctrine of *practical* reason to provide philosophical support for the validity of the intuition.

As a result, the knowledge of the imagination and intuition—the concerns of Romantic poetry—was judged as being as valid as the verifiable knowledge of the senses; and the "winged flight into the empyrean" became a trustworthy means of obtaining knowledge and of interpreting experience. The significance of Kant, then, to this study of Dowden is twofold: (1) the radical separation effected in Dowden between rationalism and religion —and poetry!—by Kant's thesis of pure reason; and (2) the closer alliance of the truth-claims of religion—and poetry—with man's ethical concerns.

Kantian philosophy made its impact in Britain in a rather indirect manner through the writings of Wordsworth and Coleridge, both of whom were attracted to this mode of thought in terms analogous to those of one of Kant's successors, F. W. J. Schelling. That the Transcendentalism of Wordsworth was analogous to that of Schelling from 1795 to 1805 has been established by E. D. Hirsch's recent publication, *Wordsworth and Schelling* (1960). And Coleridge's indebtedness, usually as it relates to his notorious plagiarisms, has been established by Thomas De Quincey, James G. Ferrier, Anna Augusta Helmholtz, René Wellek, and J. W. Beach.[2] Like Kant and his disciple Schelling, Wordsworth and Coleridge were interested in the same central problems—the nature of religious and of poetic knowledge and authority. And, like the two German philosophers, the two English poets grounded belief in the living experience of faith.

Schelling, seeking to bridge the gap left by Kant between subject and object, sought a unifying element behind Kant's categories in which the categories themselves exist—in some "common life" which would transcend the opposition between mind and matter—a oneness higher than the life of each of them in particular. Schelling followed Johann Gottlieb Fichte, also a disciple of Kant, in finding this Unity in the activity of the mind; however, unlike Fichte, Schelling gave this Unity form—ontological status —whereas Fichte understood it merely as a function.

If, then, subject and object are essential phases of a common Unity, as Schelling affirmed, how is the problem of freedom and necessity to be understood? Schelling resolved the opposition of freedom and necessity in the activity of self-determination: the opposition between the freedom one experiences within himself and the necessity that one runs counter to outside himself is overcome in the will. Necessary identity with the universal being would have no existentiality, only essentiality, thereby confirming pure idealism. Hence, in searching for the distinguishing difference between universal being and "factual, free, individual being," between absolute Ego and finite Ego, between being as subject of thought and being as existence, Schelling used "the term 'will' as sign of the highest potential individuality and the term 'to will' as the full expression of individual, factual, free existence." [3] Thus he established a dialectical duality, where, as elsewhere in his system, opposites do not exclude each other; for, while one is free to exercise his own will, he is at the same time fulfilling "Nature's holy plan." There is a "power," Schelling asserted, "by which we, even in our free activity without our knowledge, and even against our wills, realize goals unawares." [4] As a result, the unconscious intuitive nature of the individual moves in a path ordered by the universal being.

To posit thus, as Schelling did, true freedom as an essential tenet of his thought necessitated a consequent tenet of man's moral responsibility. To Schelling, the will to be something independent is the original evil of man: when consciousness denies its connections, it acts immorally. But, when the will recognizes itself as a part of nature's life, it executes the will of God and is thereby moral. For, when man harmoniously subordinates himself to the universal being and consciously becomes a part of nature's life, an irresistible force for good compels and motivates him. Such moral regeneration is effected by man's comprehension of, and his being comprehended by, the great Unity of all being: "The rebirth will necessarily begin when the divinity of Nature and the great unity of all being are again comprehended." [5] Thus, Schelling recognizes inner truth as man's ethical motivating force—as the primal factor in man's moral regeneration.

The willing union of the individual with the universal is effected, Schelling says, by imagination, the basic element of which is feeling. The imagination as such is the living copula between man and the world. Only by a "feeling-with" can he come to know the life of things. Sympathy with the concrete facts of life and commitment to that which is absolute and infinite in these facts is effected not by abstract thought but by inward feelings—by an emotional and intuitive apprehension of the kinship of all life. And only by such sympathy and commitment can man hope to bind himself in love to things and to his fellowmen; only by such a bond can man, in turn, expect peace and joy within.

With such philosophical background available for support, the English Romantics could justifiably assert in their poetry the essential reality of that which transcends the limitations of human reason and is apprehended only by the intuition: Wordsworth in his poem, "Tintern Abbey," could attest to a Presence rolling through all things, and in *The Prelude,* to one song of all things animate and inanimate:

> I felt the sentiment of Being spread
> O'er all that moves, and all that seemeth still,
> O'er all that, lost beyond the reach of thought
> And human knowledge, to the human eye
> Invisible, yet liveth to the heart;
> O'er all that leaps and runs, and shouts and sings,
> Or beats the gladsome air; o'er all that glides
> Beneath the wave, yea, in the wave itself,
> And mighty depth of waters. Wonder not
> If high the transport, great the joy I felt,
> Communing in this sort through earth and heaven
> With every form of creature, as it looked
> Towards the Uncreated with a countenance
> Of adoration, with an eye of love.
> One song they sang . . .
>
> (*The Prelude,* II, ll. 401–16)

Similarly, Coleridge in his notebooks could testify to "an Immense Being that strangely fills the soul," and in his poem, "The Eolian Harp," to the "one intellectual breeze / At once the Soul of each, and God of all," to the "one Life within us and abroad."

Concerning the dialectical resolution of the contradiction between freedom and necessity, Wordsworth could write in "A Poet! He hath put his heart to school":

> How does the Meadow-flower its bloom unfold?
> Because the lovely little flower is free
> Down to its root, and, in that freedom, bold;
> And so the grandeur of the Forest-tree
> Comes not by casting in a formal mould,
> But from its *own* divine vitality.

Coleridge could testify in "Destiny of Nations":

> For what is Freedom, but the unfettered use
> Of all the powers which God for use had given?

> But chiefly this, him First, him Last to view
> Through meaner powers and secondary things
> Effulgent, as through clouds that veil his blaze.

And in his notebooks, an entry of 1795, he could write:

> I mix in life and labor to seem free,
> With common person pleas'd and common things—
> While every Thought and action tends to thee
> And every impulse from thy Influence springs.

Both poets also recognized feeling, or intuitive insight, as man's ethical motivating force. Wordsworth wrote in *The Prelude* (I, ll. 342–43) that emotion reconciles "Discordant elements, makes them cling together / In one society." Coleridge jotted in his notebooks in 1795–96: "Optimist—by having no will but the will of Heaven we call in omnipotence to fight our battles!" In notes to a sermon to be preached in 1794, he declared that lack of fidelity to fellow creatures or to God is a breach in the inner harmony of things, a spoiling of an original communion "between each Spirit and all Spirits in their depths of Being below."

The concept that the union of the real and the ideal could be effected by intuition, by imagination, by love, and by joy finds many forms of expression in Coleridge's works: "Love transforms the souls into a conformity with the object loved" and "an immense Being does strangely fill the Soul: and Omnipotency, and Omnisciency, and Infinite Goodness do enlarge and dilate the Spirit, while it fixtly [*sic*] looks upon them. They raise strong Passions of Love and Admiration, which melt our Nature, and Transform it into the mould and image of that which we contemplate." [6]

As demonstrated, Schelling, Wordsworth, and Coleridge were profoundly influenced by the revolution in philosophy effected by Kant—a shift in epistemology that affected poets and their theories of literature. The new epistemology validated the knowledge gained by the poet who saw not only with his eyes but through them. No longer was nature a dead object with which man could have no living experience. Through the loving eye of the imagination, man could now become aware of the oneness of all things because of a spirit common to himself and to nature—a spirit—that had its source in One beyond them both by which they were united.

Besides the shift in epistemological sanctions which provided
the philosophical substratum for the Transcendental ideas of the
Romantics, there was another shift accepted by the Romantics
that is relevant to this study of Dowden, a shift that may perhaps
be described as a wild offshoot of the revolutionary alteration in
metaphysics. The new freedom and respect gained by post-
Kantian epistemology for the imagination and intuition led to ex-
plorations not only in the transempirical realms of religion and
order but also in those of fantasy and caprice such as in a fairyland graced by the presence of a Queen Mab, in ruined castles
haunted by ghouls, in horrors perpetrated by a Frankenstein, Medieval fantasies unsupported by reality, and in private visions asserted by the ego and self-will. This aspect of Romanticism Dowden rejected and censured; and two Romantic poets who were
especially culpable, he thought, were Sir Walter Scott and Lord
Byron. Though Dowden thought Scott to be a beautiful teacher,
he believed that his works were not rooted in actuality and that
his lack of spirituality deprived his books of "the highest good."
Byron's poetry was "too irresponsible an assertion of individual
freedom." [7] It asserted the supremacy of the individual will without answering how this freedom is to be used. A product of "the
great void in the world surrounding him—of faiths that had
fallen, of forces that had been spent," Byron was without a social
faith; and, as a result, he was thrown "back upon his own craving
heart and its unsanctified passions." [8]

To Dowden, those nineteenth-century writers whose emphasis
was placed exclusively on concrete fact as an object of scientific
observation became known as Realists or Naturalists; those whose
emphasis transcended the concrete fact to "Something" beyond it
by which the particular natural fact was to be understood and
interpreted were the Romantics. These two streams of intellectual
tendency—one sustaining the best of the preceding centuries to
which modern science belongs, the other developing the inheritance of the preceding epoch with a changed epistemology—
characterized nineteenth-century literature. Dowden, who attempts to be true to both of these schools of thought, seeks to
sustain the tension between these conflicting ideologies—between, on the one hand, science and realism, and, on the other
hand, poetry, religion, and Romanticism. Always he has one foot
in the sensory world of science, one in the supersensory world of

poetry and religion; one in the finite, one in the infinite world.
And, though he may shift his weight from one foot to the other, he
is never content to relinquish one in favor of the other.

II *Affinity with Transcendental Thought*

Scattered expressions throughout Dowden's poetry and prose
are tinged with Transcendental thought, which may be culled to
demonstrate his affinity with the German philosophy. Basic tenets
of Transcendentalism noticeable in his works are: (1) the concept
of the universe as "oneness"; (2) a dialectical resolution of the
contradiction between freedom and necessity; (3) the moral imperatives involved in the union of the real and the ideal; (4) the
imagination as the bond effecting the union between the real and
the ideal, the sensory and the supersensory. Because of Dowden's
fairness in giving all viewpoints an honest hearing, one finds a
tendency for the Transcendental thought that dominates his work
to dissolve into Platonic idealism, or into mysticism, or into hu-
manism; but, because of his clearly stated rejections of these and
because his expressions of Transcendental thought appear from
the earliest to the latest of his published works, his adherence
throughout his life to a Transcendental ideology is evident.

Though the evidence for Dowden's adherence to a Transcendental creed is cumulative, there are two poems—one among the
earliest of his published works; the other unpublished, the last of
his poems—which may be cited as evidence of his early and late
concern with Transcendentalism. The first, "The Secret of the
Universe (By a Western Spinning Dervish)," is grouped among
the earliest written of Dowden's works between 1867–1873:[9]

> I spin, I spin, around, around
> And close my eyes,
> And let the bile arise
> From the sacred region of the soul's Profound;
> Then gaze upon the world; how strange! how new!
> *The earth and heaven are one,*
> *The horizon-line is gone,*
> The sky how green! the land how fair and blue!
> Perplexing items fade from my large view,
> *And thought* which vexed me with its false and true
> *Is swallowed up in Intuition; this,*
> *This is the sole true mode*

Of reaching God,
And gaining the universal synthesis
Which makes All—One; while fools with peering eyes
Dissect, divide, and vainly analyze.
So round, and round, and round again!
How the whole world swells within my brain,
The stars inside my lids appear,
The murmur of the spheres I hear
Throbbing and beating in each ear;
Right in my navel I can feel
The center of the world's great wheel.
Ah peace divine, bliss dear and deep,
No stay, no stop,
Like any top
Whirling with swiftest speed, I sleep.
O yet devout ones round me coming,
Listen! I think that *I am humming;*
No utterance of the servile mind
With poor chop-logic rules agreeing
Here shall ye find,
But inarticulate burr of man's unsundered being.
Ah, could we but devise some plan,
Some patent jack *by which a man*
Might hold himself ever in harmony
With the great Whole, and spin perpetually,
As all things spin
Without, within,
As Time spins off into Eternity
And space into the inane Immensity,
And the Finite into God's Infinity.
Spin, spin, spin, spin. [Italics added]

Here is the oneness of the universe, apprehended mystically, earth
and heaven, man and nature, Time and Eternity, space and Immensity, the Finite, and Infinity—all are synthesized in the "sacred region of the soul's Profound," in the Transcendental "great
Whole." Here also is a hint of the contradiction between freedom
and necessity: "we" have a part in devising some plan by which
"we" may hold ourselves "in harmony with the great Whole."

The second, a fragmentary last poem without a title that consists of only a first stanza and a part of a second version of the
stanza, was written by Dowden only a few days before his death,
after seeing daffodils—an acre or so—in bloom in the grass:

> I have seen God's light and beauty—a new birth
> Of wonder that my soul and senses fills—
> Nor scaled the heavens—but trod enraptured earth
> And revelled with the reeling daffodils
>
> or
>
> And gazed upon the reeling daffodils
> I have seen God's light and beauty x x / –
> x x x x x x x x x x x x x x x x x x x
> Born of the Earth and Heaven x x x x [*sic*]

Admittedly, conclusions drawn from an incomplete poem must also be less than complete, but traces of an objective idealism are detectable. In the first stanza, God's light is available not to those scaling the heavens, but to those who tread the earth and revel in or gaze upon daffodils: the supersensory is in the sensory, the ideal in the real, a concept that is confirmed by the unfinished second stanza in which God's light and beauty are born of the Earth *and* Heaven, as well as by the loaded adjective in the first stanza "enraptured," which describes the earth. There is also in the first and second lines of the first stanza a suggestion of the moral regeneration effected by the discovery of the ideal in the real: the effect of seeing God's beauty in gazing upon daffodils is a "new birth" which is characterized by an accompanying "wonder" that fills the soul and senses.

Hence, the last poem ever written by Dowden displays, like one of his earliest, the Transcendentalist concepts of the oneness of the universe and of the moral regeneration effected by recognition of that unity. Though both of these poems are oriented in a Transcendental dialectic, there is a striking difference between them, a difference which goes straight to the core of Dowden's thought, and one which provoked to some extent, as has been noted, Dowden's aloofness from the revival of Irish legend and folklore led by such mystics as George Russell and W. B. Yeats. The irony of the first poem contrasts with the simple sincerity of the second. If an analysis is made of its charged phrases and clauses, the first poem seems intended as satire: "I . . . close my eyes, And let the bile arise"; "the whole world swells within my brain"; "The stars inside my lids appear"; "Ah peace divine, . . . Like any top / Whirling with swiftest speed, I sleep"—all are tinged with irony. Also, the Transcendental insights attributed to the spinning dervish of the first poem are gained in a different manner from those won by the initiate of the "enraptured earth" of the second poem. The spinning Mohammedan friar's vision evolved from his "brain" with closed eyes, from his own "bile." "Thought" for him is "swallowed up in Intuition"; those unlike him who "dissect, divide, and . . . analyze" are considered as "fools with peering eyes"; that is, the approach of the dervish to reality was exclusively subjective. On the other hand, the truth of "God's light and beauty" in the second poem was apprehended by *both* the "soul" *and* the "senses" of the initiate—by both intuition and thought (or in Coleridge's terms, by both reason and understanding. The subjective idealism of the Mohammedan friar, Dowden would have considered illusory, fantastic, egocentric; the objective idealism of the initiate of the second poem he himself approved.

These two poems are exemplary of the large amount of material available in Dowden's works which indicate his concern with the Transcendental. Though the examples given are poetry, which was not Dowden's chief contribution to literature, the thought expressed in them is essential rather than accidental. If Mrs. Dowden's estimate of her husband is accepted—and there is no reason to doubt it—one finds in Dowden's verse "a part of himself which never found complete issue in prose and which was his most real self." [10]

III   *The Universe as "Oneness"*

The basic tenet of Transcendental thought in Dowden's works that must be considered is that of the universe as Oneness. This concept is phrased variously in his works: "the Whole of things," "the Soul of the World," "that Supreme Reality," "that Supreme Power," "some higher Being or Law," "the great totality of being." Dowden's awareness, contact, and participation with this "Soul of the World" takes place chiefly, though not exclusively, when he is alone with the phenomena of Nature. The beauties of the landscape around Dublin, a solitary morning on Bray Head, or a stroll to Howth seem to create in him the necessary mood of exaltation for conscious participation with the "Supreme Reality" found in, with, and under natural phenomena. Records of such experience appear in his poetry and letters.

In an undated poem in his volume of *Poems,* entitled "The Inner Life, I. A Disciple," Dowden contrasts the effects of seeking "God" through religion and through nature to the advantage of the latter: not theologians but a "brook" reveals to him "the world's Light" which is his own Light and Life:

> Master, they argued fast concerning Thee,
> Proved what Thou art, denied what Thou art not,
> Till brows were on the fret, and eyes grew hot,
> And lip and chin were thrust out eagerly;
> Then through the temple-door I slipped to free
> My soul from secret ache in solitude,
> And sought this brook, and by the brookside stood
> The world's Light, and the Light and Life of me.
> It is enough, O Master, speak no word!
> The stream speaks, and the endurance of the sky
> Outpasses speech: I seek not to discern
> Even what smiles for me Thy lips have stirred;
> Only in Thy hand still let my hand lie,
> And let the musing soul within me burn.

In another poem, entitled "Ritualism," the out-of-doors is compared to a cathedral where "God Himself" is not only being worshipped by the natural phenomena, but *is* natural phenomena— "God Himself being bread and wine":

> This is high ritual and a holy day;
> I think from Palestrina the wind chooses
> That movement in the firs; one sits and muses
> In hushed near-vacancy made meek to pray;
> Listen! the birds are choristers with gay
> Clear voices infantile, and with good will
> Each acolyte flower has swung his thurible,
> Censing to left and right these aisles of May.
> For congregation, see real sheep most clean,
> And I—what am I, worshipper or priest?
> At least all these I dare absolve from sin,
> Ay, dare ascend to where the splendours shine
> Of yon mountain-altar, and the feast
> Is holy, God Himself being bread and wine.

Also in "At Mullion" and in "The Invitation" nature is a cathedral, the beneficence of which is universal light and benediction for all. In both of these poems there is an illumination and absolution that the initiate of nature's ritual experiences:

At Mullion (Cornwall)
Sunday

Where the blue dome is infinite,
And choral voices of the sea
Chaunt the high lauds, or meeks, as now,
Intone their ancient litany;

Where through his ritual pomp still moves
The Sun robe pontifical,
Whose only creed is catholic light,
Whose benediction is for all;

I enter with glad face uplift,
As purged on brow and brain and heart;
I am confessed, absolved, illumed,
Receive my blessing and depart.

Similarly, the second speaker in the brief lyric, "Speakers to God"
identifies God not only as the union of the sky's rim and ocean's
rim but also as the sea:

Speakers to God
Second Speaker

I am borne out to thee upon the wave,
And the land lessens; cry nor speech I hear,
Nought but the leaping waters and the brave
Pure winds commingling. O the joy, the fear!

Alone with thee: sky's rim and ocean's rim
Touch, overhead the clear immensity
Is merely God; no eyes of seraphim
Gaze in . . . O God, Thou also art the sea!

In a letter to Miss West, dated October 22, 1872, Dowden described such contact with the Eternal as a moral change or a re-
generative influence that made him desire to renounce evil forever.

Because of a feeling of being wafted from this earth to the
empyrean—of a sense of the unreality of the external world—
inherent in these experiences and characteristic of them, they suggest a pattern of thought related to Platonic idealism, an appre-

hension of man's experience which, though not completely uncongenial to Dowden, was finally rejected by him. In 1871, he wrote: "There is no matter in the universe. In tasting a peach we are engaged in a spiritual service, and are in the immediate presence of the most Divine. Every sensation and every thought leads into an immeasurable abyss of Deity." [11] In 1872, he expressed again his uncertainty of belief as to the existence of an external world: "Surely uncertainties of belief about the existence of an external world must remain." [12] In 1873, a walk with his friends J. B. Yeats and Wilson to Howth provoked the same thought: "We walked along the cliff. It was a day when one can believe the external world unreal and as curious an apparition as our mysterious friend the sea, but under all the show of things abode and always abides, one strong reality and blessedness, as solid now as when the last lines of 'The Testing-Place (A Howth Poem)' were written." [13]

In a poem, entitled "From April to October, I. Beauty," he described beauty in abstract Platonic terms. The pools, clouds, buds, leaves, lizards, stars, and sea—all are but figures in the garb, the veil of beauty:

> The beauty of the world, the loveliness
> Of woodland pools, which doves have coo'd to sleep
> Dreaming the noontide through beneath the deep
> Of heaven; the radiant blue's benign caress
> When April clouds are rifted; buds that bless
> Each little nook and bower, where the leaves keep
> Dew and light shadow, and quick lizards peep
> For sunshine,—these, and the ancient stars no less
> And the sea's mystery of dusk and bright
> Are but the curious characters that lie,
> Priestess of Beauty, in thy robe of light.
> Ah, where, divine One, is thy veiled retreat,
> That I may creep to it and clasp thy feet,
> And gaze in thy pure face though I should die?

In 1886, he confessed in a letter: "Facts and history often seem to me mere bags of shadows which darken and burden us in our flight towards 'the only permanent shore. . . . The cape never rounded or wandered o'er.'" [14] In 1901, he reluctantly admitted, though *"less sure,"* that the senses cooperate with the reason.

But there are direct rejections of this type of idealism that Dowden himself recorded. Once, when Miss West called him an idealist, he replied: "I accept your statement that I am an idealist myself, except with large reserves. What I will admit is that I *should* be an idealist if I had not been finding my way ever more and more into the real facts of life, and now I am an idealist transformed by the touch of life into a most determined seeker for fact." [15] Though somewhat appealing to Dowden, an idealism divorced from the real, concrete facts of life was an illusory system of thought, a foolishly inadequate notion. The "ideal Whole"—a term by which Dowden understood the Oneness of the universe—when *subjectively* conceived was a vacuous abstraction which erroneously disregarded externality, an understanding of reality not close to the sensory world; and those authors whose apprehension of the universe was strictly subjective erred. Victor Hugo's idealism and William Godwin's rationalistic dogma, for example, were one-sided because not sobered through concrete experience. Subjective truth, such as these men held, was only a fragment of truth. Hence, the only kind of idealism with which Dowden was congenial was one informed with the concrete facts of life: an objective idealism.

As well as in terms of idealism, Dowden clothes his enrapturing and transfiguring experiences with the "Soul of the World" in terms of mysticism; the senses and the rational intellect are not the media through which the transfiguration comes about, nor are words sufficient to contain or communicate the mystery of the encounter with Reality. In the lyric "In the Mountains," Dowden's enraptured spirit was as though it were bodiless; and words lacked power to portray the intensity of the vision (ll. 45–51). Also, in recounting the rapture that was his in hearing "Life's ecstasy" from the waning of the morning star in another lyric, "The Morning Star," he described the rapturous song and flame of the star as being from the "altars of the universe," as being "too deep for thought, too bright for dim investiture of mortal words." The sundering of the flesh from the spirit, as it were, depicts the poet's apprehending of the supersensory also in "The Initiation." In it, the apocalyptic vision transports the seer from time to eternity; and he questions how he came back to earth after his vision. Moreover, one finds that the vision effects a moral renewal—"My sight is purged; I love and pity men":

Under the flaming wings of cherubim
I moved toward that high altar. O, the hour!
And the light waxed intenser, and the dim
Low edges of the hills and the grey sea
Were caught and captur'd by the present Power
My sureties and my witnesses to be.

Then the light drew me in. Ah, perfect pain!
Ah, infinite moment of accomplishment!
Thou terror of pure joy, with neither wane
Nor waxing, but long silence and sharp air
As womb-forsaking babes breathe. Hush! the event
Let him who wrought Love's marvellous things declare.

Shall I who fear'd not joy, fear grief at all?
I on whose mouth Life laid his sudden lips
Tremble at Death's weak kiss, and not recall
That sundering from the flesh, the flight from time,
The judgments stern, the clear apocalypse,
The lightnings, and the Presences sublime.

How came I back to earth? I know not how,
Nor what hands led me, nor what words were said.
Now all things are made mine,—joy, sorrow; now
I know my purpose deep and can restrain;
I walk among the living not the dead;
My sight is purged; I love and pity men.

In "The Top of a Hill Called Clear," Dowden's experience is one
of a spiritual rebirth attended by absolute joy and love, one in
which will is "made sane"—an experience which "no words" may
"hold fast":

New life,—not death! No glow the senses cast
Across the spirit, no pleasure shoot o'er me
Its scattering flaw, no words may I hold fast
Here, where God's breath streams inexhaustibly;
But conquest stern is mine, a will made sane,
Life's vision wide and calm, a supreme pain,
An absolute joy; and love the first and last.

But Dowden's grasp of the concrete is as determined as that of
the empyrean; in earthly skies are seen divine lightnings. "A man

does not attain to the universal," he wrote,[16] "by abandoning the particular, nor to the everlasting by an endeavor to overleap the limitations of time and place. The abiding reality exists not somewhere apart in the air, but under certain temporary and local forms of thought, feeling, and endeavor." Nature and man are manifestations of the "Supreme Power, unknown yet well known." For man to ignore, or fail to discuss, a higher Being or law to which the individual members belong brings chaos. Mere observation of a castle in Scotland, erected by the controlled forces of human will, leads Dowden to reflections of "power unowned of sense, / Presences awful, vast, and uncontrolled."[17]

In the brief poem "Among the Rocks," Dowden asked himself if the Prime Force is the accretion of collective humanity or if it is that "something" the existence of which is to be identified with the source of things. The answer to his question is surely given in his essay on "Tennyson and Browning" in *Studies in Literature*, in which he clearly affirmed that culture is inadequate to satisfy the total needs of man—self-reverence, self-knowledge, self-control— if it is separated from recognition of a divine order and of one's own place in that order. Similarly, he stated in his *History of French Literature* that a philosophy of culture, such as Voltaire's, which ignores the supernatural is a "sad little philosophy of existence," "a grave defect," "a blindness to the significance of religious phenomena." What Dowden needed was real powers transcending the projected idealizations of man, transcending man himself, collective or individual. To use a traditional word for such power, Dowden felt he needed "God."

Though occasionally called "God" by Dowden, the inscrutable Power or Force of his religiously oriented thought is not the God of organized religion—either of Judaism or of Christianity—but the God beyond this God: "All nineteenth-century poetry— Wordsworth, Goethe, Shelley—seems to me to become theistic in its higher moods of nature-worship; but the God is not the Jehovah of Mount Sinai, nor the amiable white-bearded old gentleman of Catholic pictorial art, nor the constitutional ruler governing by general laws of Protestantism, but the true God (of which these are figures), the God of the Ethics of Spinoza; in whom, as one of your poets says, we live and move and have our being."[18]

The only type of Christianity to which Dowden was finally attracted, therefore was the liberal Protestant Christianity such as

Frederick Denison Maurice set forth. A transcendental type of Christianity, it was heavily indebted to the influence of Samuel Taylor Coleridge. Though Maurice never met Coleridge, he did more than any other man to spread the message of Coleridge throughout Victorian England. When Maurice was at Trinity College, Cambridge, he had defended Coleridge's metaphysics against the cold rationalism of Utilitarianism. While there, Maurice also credited to Coleridge's metaphysics his own preservation from infidelity. And the characteristic ideas of the one man appear in the works of the other. Through his disciple Maurice, Coleridge provided a new method into the discussion of Christian theology.

Coleridge insisted that the imagination and senses of man are as necessary as the rational processes to the apprehension of reality. Coleridge, and Maurice after him, was still a rationalist in a sense; yet his distinction between Reason and Understanding made him a rationalist with a difference. Reason, Coleridge believed, was not only the organ of the phenomenal but of the supersensory; it was the inner eye of the spirit by which one directly apprehends truth, the knowledge of the Oneness of all things. Understanding, on the other hand, was the faculty by which one generalizes and arranges the phenomena of perception.

Following Coleridge, Maurice argued for the apprehension of reality, not with "mere calculating understanding," but with deep "feelings and passions." Upon this Coleridgean doctrine Maurice based his faith in every man's ability to penetrate into the supersensory, a faith that promised to make religion vital again for the masses and that had strong appeal to Dowden: "Maurice . . . seems to me to have sunk down upon the real solid realities of life," wrote Dowden, "and to rest upon the very truth. . . . One feels that he has attained reality." [19] Maurice declared a "oneness" of the universe from the beginning of things, a perfect harmony that already exists in the universe, a natural relationship of man as divine to God the Father, as revealed to mankind through the Atonement of Christ. The Atonement was the revelation of how things really are: men *are* in the divine image; they *have* God as their Father; each of the race is, therefore, vitally connected with the divine.

Because the immediate reality of Dowden's experience of God transcended the bounds of religious formulae, the careful definition of the Incarnation and the Atonement as spun out by Maurice would have been absorbed by Dowden but as accidental, rather than as essential, to his view. To Dowden, Christ, like "every good and perfect gift in the world, is God manifest, the manifestation of God in man, differing, however, only in degree not in kind from His other manifestations." [20]

Dowden believed Maurice to be more accurate in his attempts to ascertain truth because, in an effort to reach the divine, he did not deny the human concrete facts of life; instead, Maurice found the divine in the human:

We can imagine the pain with which Mr. Maurice would have heard himself styled "transcendental" but presently that most sympathetic of adversaries would doubtless have discovered that you were right, only in his sense, not your own; "transcendental," yes, because before all else needing some realities, some abiding facts, and not theories about facts; "transcendental," then, because above everything a realist. Mr. Maurice's theology, as a recent critic, the Reverend James Martineau, has observed, is at once an effort to oppose the pantheistic tendency, and is itself reached and touched by that tendency. How to connect the human and the divine had been a question since the transition from eighteenth-century thought had been effected. . . . Mr. Maurice answered that there is a divine life in the world, a kingdom of God in process of advancement, a divine centre and head of humanity; in the infinite, divine life each one of us participates; with the divine head of our race each one is vitally connected; "all the higher human relations are but faint echoes of relations already existing in an infinitely more perfect form in the divine mind"; the higher movement of society, the spiritual tides of passion and of thought, the cry in our century for freedom and for order, the search in our century for certitude, for light, all these are portions of that life of God in the world which manifests itself most conspicuously in the incarnation and the life of a Son of Man who is also a Son of God! . . . The new theologians translated Christianity out of time into eternity; they read in the life and death of Christ no scheme, no plot with astonishing catastrophe; but the symbol and sample of constant divine life with men, and of human sonship to God, disclosing relations which had for ever been and would for ever be; only adding now the glad surprise that the sigh for better life, the response of conscience to high appeals, the inward sympathy with all righteousness, are not lonely visions, but the personal communion of the perfect with the imperfect mind.[21]

"Transcendental," then, was a word to Dowden which included not only that which transcended sensory knowledge but also that which required sensory realities—not theories about realities but real, concrete facts. It was to Maurice that Dowden attributed a solution adequate to the problem of connecting the faith of the Romantics in their ability to apprehend truth by way of the feelings and imagination with the Positivism of the scientists in their reliance on empirically verifiable facts, both of which kinds of knowledge were bequeathed separately to Dowden, as well as to all other Victorians. The facts discovered by the scientists were to be considered as enlargements of man's sphere of apprehension of even greater realities beyond the empirical data itself, Dowden affirmed in "The Scientific Movement and Literature." The religious spirit of man is to be fed by all that can be known in the laboratory of man, but "around and beyond what is knowable will abide an encircling mystery."

Thus, Dowden, while not denying the empirical method of the scientists, confirms that the intellect, or reason, is not the sole source of truth. That reconciliation of the conflict between head-and-heart knowledge, one which would deny neither the one nor the other but sustain both, was, according to Dowden, to be found by a Transcendental dialectic; and for this reason Dowden favorably commented on Maurice who, like his philosophical progenitor Coleridge, found the Divine in life, the invisible captured by the visible.

Dowden's Transcendental tendencies evidence a derivation more directly from Wordsworth. Maurice and Coleridge are mentioned only a handful of times by Dowden, but he makes frequent mention of Wordsworth as a decisive influence in his thinking. Wordsworth possessed Dowden in his growing years almost to the exclusion of all other influences, declared his widow and former editor and collaborator. Admiration for Wordsworth was considered by Dowden to be a hallmark of excellent character in the admirer.

Wordsworth, more than any other of the nineteenth century, offered to his fellowmen, Dowden believed, "a harmony on the whole as much in keeping with our condition as any that has been offered to our hearing," [22] a resolution which was similarly Dowden's concern. The forces of Wordsworth's mind were correlated by a law bringing about an "entire consentaneity of thought and feeling"—neither pure thought nor pure passion preceding or initiating the movement of the other; but thought informing feelings, and feeling informing thought. To Wordsworth the matter-of-factness of life was inspired by the divine illumination; and the real and the ideal were not opposed but resolved in harmony, each submitting to the influence of the other: "The skyey splendours take a somber colouring; the things of use and wont become more precious because more habitually informed with what is spiritual." [23] The Divine is operative in the human: "in the instincts of human nature, in hope, in fortitude, in martyrdom, lives and moves the supreme Power of the universe." [24] Wordsworth's contribution to his contemporaries was a persuasive apprehension of the permanent principles of human nature, the validity of which Dowden felt to be of "no less worth . . . for our day than they were for the opening days of the century." [25]

What caused the occasional fluctuations of loyalty in Dowden to Wordsworthian influence was Wordsworth's tendency to remove himself from reality, to idealize away the facts of life, to oppose the scientific method of observation. An unnamed friend of Wordsworth's wrote that he remembered "Mr. Wordsworth saying that, at a particular stage of his mental progress, he used to be frequently so rapt into an unreal transcendental world of ideas that the external world seemed no longer to exist in relation to him, and he had to reconvince himself of the existence by clasping a tree, or something that happened to be near him." [26] Such an obscurantist tendency was a cause for concern in Dowden's regard for the great Romantic. That is, when Wordsworth thus retreated into his own vision of truth rather than oriented this truth into fruitful relation with fact, his ideas tended to become abstract, private, and notional; then, since only partially related to things as they are, his concepts were less moving as an "announcement of truth transcendental."

Though Wordsworth was perhaps the first and most thoroughgoing influence towards Dowden's Transcendental thought, Fichte, Hans Christian Oersted, and Johann Wolfgang von Goethe, other Continental scholars contributing to and influenced by German idealism, should also be mentioned. As early as 1864, Dowden had read Fichte's *Destination of Man*. In his essay, "The Transcendental Movement and Literature," he acknowledged in a footnote the debt of English Transcendentalism to German philosophical speculation. Dowden had also read Hans Oersted's *Der Geist in der Natur* (*The Spirit in Nature*), two chapters of which he especially recommended in a footnote to his essay, "The Scientific Movement and Literature": "Über das Verhältnis zwischen der Natur-Auffassung des Denkens unter der Einbildungskraft" ("Concerning the Relationship Between The Nature-Concept of Thought in Imagination") and "Das Verhältnis der Naturwissenschaft zur Dichtkunst" ("The Relation of Science and Literature").

A Danish scientist and Professor of Physics at the University of Copenhagen, Oersted spent several years in Germany in friendly relationship with Schelling, the Schlegel brothers, Fichte, and other German celebrities of the era. Oersted deals with the two different approaches of the human mind towards nature, the scientific and the imaginative or poetic. These two approaches, pursued separately for centuries, need not be antagonistic, Oersted asserts, but may interrelate their functions. The wonderful field of astronomy offers a rich reward for a combined approach, for the scientific and poetic approaches most often converge in the starry world. Oersted is of the opinion that poets do not have to stick with old expressions which contradict scientific insights. Against both the exclusive supernaturalism of the theologians and the strict fanatic empiricism of the scientist, Oersted believed the two met in "*den Mittelpunkt Vernunftreich der grossen Einheit aller Gedanken, die würdigere Gotteskenntnis in Auge, zu welcher alle Wege de Gedanken führen mussen*" ("midpoint realm of reason of the great Unity of all thoughts, the more worthy knowledge of God in view, to which all paths of thought must lead). Oersted's contribution, then, was his stress on the importance and role of the subconscious to the conscious self: Oersted "*geht mehr den intuitiv-philosophischen Weg*" ("takes the more intuitive philosophical approach").

Dowden's attraction to Goethe will be discussed in the next chapter.

IV   *A Dialectical Resolution of the Contradictions between Freedom and Necessity*

After considering the first basic tenet of Transcendental thought appearing in Dowden's works—the universe as Oneness —one should consider a second aspect of his thought, the dialectical resolution of necessity and freedom; for it, too, is influenced by Transcendentalism. If the universe is "Oneness," then there may be implied a denial of freedom in favor of predetermination: an individual cannot choose to do other than move along with the "Oneness"; he is externally compelled. In "Oneness," there may thus be implied a commitment to necessary identity of the particular with the universal, and hence, a consequent dissolution of the polarity between freedom and necessity. The distinction between freedom and necessity Dowden sought to maintain. By such dialectical duality Dowden would be enabled to explain, for example, the individual genius of the artist and the universal mind of humanity, the existence of evil along with the good, and the imperfect though maturing nature of man.

Freedom of the human will is expressed variously in his works, frequently in connection with the French Revolution, a cataclysm with more constructive consequences than destructive ones—in Dowden's estimation. To him, the cry for freedom from oppressing tyrants, from decadent creed, and from discredited tradition was negative and destructive. Also, some of the beliefs supporting its energies were illusory: the belief in the perfectibility of man, the disregard of tradition and inheritance, the contrast between a benevolent Nature and the selfishness of Society—these were illusions of the Revolution, though admittedly "generous illusions." But the Revolution was also constructive in character in its enthusiasm for humanity, its passion for justice, its recognition of a moral element in politics, and its sentiment about the brotherhood of man—these were admirable aspects of the Revolution. Constructively, the Revolution was more of an evolution of the human race than a revoluton; it was a movement aimed at a more complete development of manhood.

The freedom valued by Dowden in the Revolution is not one to destroy but to construct; it is a freedom limited by responsibility to higher laws of life than mere assertion of personal will; it is also a freedom consonant with nature, if " 'nature' be understood to include the action of the higher part of our humanity." He suggested here that human liberty is the freedom of cultured manhood. Order, to some extent, becomes equated with God in man, with the supernatural in the natural; and obedience to this order constitutes true freedom, an outward evidence of which is a cultured society. Even the scientific contributions of culture—if "spiritual order" informed their freedom—could not but contribute to human welfare. Dowden would align himself, therefore, with

Schiller and Goethe who believed that freedom was attained
"through an education which may seem severe and even repres-
sive, yet which shall serve the cause of freedom in the end by
delivering from the vagueness and error and confusion of life that
true humanity which lies encumbered within each one of us." [27]
Ideals must be discovered among men, not in abstract concepts
but in the spatial-temporal facts of life.

Though Dowden was intensely humanistic in his concern for
the betterment of man, he always found it difficult not to go beyond merely human sanctions. The success of the ancient artists,
for instance, he credits to their being, as it were, "upon the track
of nature"—nature which, by a quote from Goethe, he identifies
with necessity or God: "'These high works of art,'" writes
Goethe, "'are also the highest works of Nature, produced by men
in accordance with true and natural laws. All arbitrariness, all
self-conceit is banished; here is necessity, here is God.'" [28]

In one sense, a man is free to cooperate with the divine law; in
an equal sense, man is carried along by the law. Each is expressive
of one portion of a truth. There is a reciprocal relationship between freedom and necessity sensed by man in himself; he feels as
though he were both actor and agent. This idea of voluntary com-
pulsion Dowden expressed in his lyric "Nature's Need":

> We are two foam-flakes on a stream,
> Two thistle-downs upon the air;
> Yet joy is therefore not a dream;
> Bear us, glad Power, we know not where!

The "two foam-flakes" joyously petition the "glad Power" to bear
them as though they had freedom to determine their involuntary
progression. The dualistic aspect of this truth seems to be the
theme of Dowden's poem "Heroines: Atalanta." After Milanion
had legitimately contested and won Atalanta, she went to the
woods rebellious but returned submissive. Several years later, she
recounts her experience to her husband:

> On the grass at last I lay
> Seized by a peace divine, I know not how;
> Passive, yet never so possessed of power,
> Strong, yet content to feel not use my strength

> Sustained a babe upon the breasts of life
> Yet armed with adult will, a shining spear.
> O strong deliverance of the larger law
> Which strove not with the less! impetuous youth
> Caught up in ampler force of womanhood!
> Co-operant ardours of joined lives! the calls
> Of heart to heart in chase of strenuous deeds!
> Virgin and wedded freedom not disjoined,
> And loyal married service to my Queen!

What Atalanta had learned is that only through submission to duty could she find true freedom—"Virgin and wedded freedom [are] not disjoined." Only through acceptance of limitation comes real expansion: true freedom is discoverable only in submitting willingly to necessity. The truth of this lesson is "the most important lesson of life," one which Dowden says Goethe learned during the ten years of service at Weimar. During this decade of service Goethe had written in his diary: "*Bestimmteres Gefühl von Einschränkung und dadurch der wahren Ausbreitung*" ("a more definite sense of limitation and thereby real expansion"). True freedom is one with the limitations of duty, limitations which, in Dowden's sense, are endowed with divine sanctions.

Any other conception of freedom leads into inferior, or even anarchical, action, such as Godwin's or Byron's unbounded freedoms. The anarchical nature of their concept of freedom, for instance, is evident in their self-will and self-esteem; for each placed his complete trust in the individual reason, a solipsistic intellectual abstraction which Dowden indicted. Godwin's doctrine was too inverted, too much removed from the facts of life, and too little mindful of one aspect of the human condition—the permanent truth of the passions. Godwin's intellect was too narrow; his imagination too contracted; his attitude too egoistic. His doctrine, which erroneously gave unlimited freedom to the individual reason, encouraged moral anarchy. He followed the eighteenth-century analytical method even in his apprehension and presentation of morality, and, bound to a deductive type of reasoning, this analytic power inhibited his imagination.[29]

Immediately following Dowden's discussion of Godwin, he calls the attention of his reader to Wordsworth's commendable delivery of himself from Godwin's narrow lessons. He recalls that in an early tragedy entitled *The Borderers* Wordsworth had identified his own salvation with a precious moment in the dramatic action in which a kindhearted youth is led to crime by the casuistic reasoning of an older man who by persuasive, though fallacious, logic brings about the disintegration of the youth's natural feelings and habitual moral checks by having him substitute a reliance on private reason. Wordsworth, who recoiled in alarm from such specious reasoning, sought in the Preface to *Lyrical Ballads* to vindicate the natural affections of mankind. In this way Dowden arraigns Godwin's doctrine for its lopsidedness.

Byron, according to Dowden, also had a warped understanding of freedom. Born in the year 1788, Byron grew up in the aftermath of the French Revolution; and the enthusiasms of the abstract doctrines of that event—Progress, Fraternity, Freedom, and Equality—animated his own soul to creative incarnation of them into poetry. His enthusiasms were affiliated, however, with the destructive forces of the Revolution rather than with the constructive instincts of his own spirit; therefore, they were the immediate cause of the internal conflict which characterized his experience— the clash within him between "light and darkness." Byron's failure to discover existential significance in his ideas led to the cynicism of his major poems, *Childe Harold* and *Don Juan,* which attest not only to the revolutionary ardor that motivated Byron but also to the moral void left by his loss of faith. Both poems exhibit scorn for human existence and bitterly mock the society that helped to make the poet scornful.

To Dowden, Byron's scorn and cynicism derive from his incapacity to believe even for a moment in what Dowden considers the constancies of life: love, fidelity, and virtue. In fact, Byron discovered that one part of himself was at war with another, the basest self at war with the more noble self. Never successful in effecting a reconciliation between the warring elements of his nature, Byron uncannily diagnosed his condition in several lines in *Manfred* that could well serve as his epitaph:

> This should have been a noble creature; he
> Hath all the energy which would have made
> A goodly frame of glorious elements,
> Had they been wisely mingled: as it is
> It is an awful chaos, and passions and pure thought
> Mix'd and contending without end or order.

Yet Byron was not without hope of redemption to Dowden: Byron's very cynicism, Dowden believed, should have revealed to him that man must live by faith; his bitterness of spirit should have informed him of the impossibility of moving joyously in a moral void. Fortunately, his contact with Shelley at the time of writing *Childe Harold* had some salutary effect, for he was thus brought under the influence of Wordsworth. Wordsworth's belief in a universal presence inhering in all things modulated Byron's song, elevating it with a natural piety, one marred indeed by his characteristic egotism, yet one purer and more refined than he had hitherto expressed or felt.[30]

Several attitudes of Dowden toward Byron are clearly presented in these passages, all of which figure in his overall estimate of the revolutionary poet. Byron's defective understanding of what true freedom consists was due, Dowden says, to his dramatic definition of freedom as an assertion of the individual will and to his lack of commitment to any order of belief that might give guidance to the will. The order of belief that Byron lacked had characteristics of "love, constancy, patriotism, virtue." With these, freedom becomes morally informed; it relates not primarily to egoism and self-will but to a self-sacrificing love.

Throughout Dowden's discussions of the subject of freedom, there are noticeable two aspects of freedom which came into focus as a result of the French Revolution: one is characterized by self-will, self-assertion generated by private reasoning, somewhat atheistic and destructive; the other is distinguished by a willing submission to laws inherent in the individual and common to society at large—laws that are at once human, divine, and constructive. As demonstrated, Dowden adhered to the divine and constructive; for he clearly affirmed that "no necessary truth is a matter of mere private judgment, but belongs to a common order of thought . . . and that this common, necessary order of thought is God manifest in the intellect." [31] Thus, the man who fails to acknowledge the greater Law by asserting his own will becomes destructive.

In some way such a man by self-assertion dissevers himself from the common order of things. Only by a willing surrender of himself to the beneficent powers outside himself can he heal the breach made by such self-assertion. The surrender is not "an enervating resignation," not a superstitious asceticism to iron necessity

such as Stoicism; it is instead, a brave "adventure of working out
an infinite amount of good from one's permanent and limited environment." [32] As Dowden interprets Wordsworth's *Ode to Duty,*
the resignation to necessity is "not law merely imposed from without; it is law within; it is free will made wise." [33]

V *The Moral Imperatives Involved in the Union of the Real and the Ideal*

A third aspect of Dowden's thought that relates him to the German Transcendentalists concerns the moral imperatives involved
in the union of the real and the ideal. The divine necessity, or
order inherent in the universe, moves toward ethical goals "as if
God had poised a soul and then flung it forward as a flaming
spear against the mark." In a sense, man plays no part in the realization of these goals; for "the hiss of the spear in mid air is hardly
a lyric cry." There is a point at which man feels he is not initiating
his own will but is being moved by extraneous powers of good; he
has a sense of strength greater than his own, of something benevolent and truth-discovering at work in him in addition to his own
faculties: "He who hath won / Life's gain doth hold ought fast,
who could hold all, / Holden himself of strong, immortal Powers." [34] "One seems to be in the possession of something . . . a
something applied to one than properly one's own, held, as it were
for one by the blessed powers of the world." [35]

Yet, in another sense, man himself brings about the realization
of moral goals: at the same time that he himself is "holden of
strong, immortal Powers," he has also "*won* Life's gain." Even as
he is carried along towards those goals, he also contributes something towards their realization. There is a reciprocal action between Nature and man, a joyous cooperation with Nature. Man's
part is to bring freely his own nature into correspondence with
the order extant in the universe.

The effect of man's freely willing the divine necessity is a feeling of harmony with his fellows and with nature, a "breathing of
the Whole of things that brings with it a mood of joy or happiness." "A creature's spiritual life depends on the real correspondence with his nature and his *milieu.* Growth proves such a correspondence, and death its absence. I must suppose then, that in
moments of faith and imaginative vision, such men are most truly
in harmony with the facts outside themselves." [36] Such a joyous

apprehension of the oneness of man and nature expresses itself naturally in continued and conscious service to others, a self-sacrifice that is indeed "joy beyond joy." If such self-sacrifice is ascetic, then it is so in the best sense of that word, in a sense of "heroic discipline" that subordinates the lower parts to the higher so that they may be strong for service. The effect of a society of men freely bringing into realization the divine necessity is, indeed, the highest expression of civil liberty and of a cultured humanity.

The effect is also a new sympathy with the things of nature, such as Coleridge's Ancient Mariner experienced:

Nor are his strange creatures of the sea those hideous worms which a vulgar dealer in the supernatural might have invented. Seen in a great calm by the light of the moon these creatures of God are beautiful in the joy of their life:—

> "Blue, glossy green, and velvet black,
> They coil'd and swam; and every track
> Was a flash of golden fire."

And it is through a sudden well-forth of sympathy with their happiness, and a sudden sense of their beauty, that the spell which binds the afflicted mariner is snapped. That one self-centred in crude egoism should be purified and converted through a new sympathy with suffering and sorrow is a common piece of morality; this purification through sympathy with joy is a piece of finer and higher doctrine.[37]

Even the inanimate things of nature are discovered as a part of that Life which informs both man and nature; in some sense the "Sea-rocks," for instance, are "kin" to man:[38]

> Never can we be strangers you and I
> Nor quite disown our mysteries of kin,
> Grey Sea-rocks, since I sat an hour today
> Companion of the ocean and of you—

The "Whole of things" is essentially good and at the same time striving toward the realization of good: "Some people find a guarantee in the evils of this world for a better state hereafter; I rather feel that because this world is in its essence good, so will be all worlds which proceed from it, and progressively better because this world is, I think, as far as it is spirit, working out the evil."[39]

The problem of suffering, sorrow, and evil is resolved, thus, in understanding them as necessary counterparts to the goodness of the Whole of things—as atoms essential to the growing Whole, whose virtue lies in their vitality, not their completeness. They are, therefore, right. Only when they are caused by man's lack of recognition of the Whole of things and by his lack of acceptance of his position in that Whole do they become arbitrary. Only when they are the fruits of man acting in separation from the Whole, do they become immoral disconnections from the totality.

Failure to feel the "divinity in man" was the cause of Iago's great crime, for example.[40] There is "something in right doing which takes it out of time" and relates it to a "more absolute kind of morality than any other." [41] When man is constrained by the powers of Good, he seems to be in possession of something which goes beyond time—a more absolute kind of morality than any other. "The evil seems a set of self-conflicting accidents; but the good authenticates itself as the law—the absolute thing," an absolute which seeks to realize itself in time.[42] To Dowden, there is a "soul of goodness in things evil"; and there is more "divine wisdom" in this view than in that "less comfortable view which passionately recognizes in evil things their essential soul of evil." [43] In his poem "La Révélation Par Le Désert," Evil and Good are comates; God and the Serpent are each necessary, one to the other:

> Is this the secret lying round the world?
> A Dread One watching with unlidded eye
> Slow century after century from his heaven,
> And that great lord, the worm of the red plain,
> Cold in mid sun, strenuous, untameable,
> Coiling his solitary strength along
> Slow century after century, conscious each
> How in the life of his Arch-enemy
> He lives, how ruin of one confounds the pair
> Is this the eternal dual mystery?
> One Source of being, Light or Love, or Lord,
> Whose shadow is the brightness of the world,
> Still let thy dawns and twilights glimmer pure
> In flow perpetual from hill to hill,
> Still bathe us in thy tides of day
> Wash me at will a weed in thy free wave
> Drenched in the sun and air and surge of Thee.

As Dowden finds the divine in both man and things, as well as a reciprocal relationship between necessity and freedom, so does he connect man's temporal striving after good with eternal, absolute goodness. Goodness, though partaking of the limitations of time, is also eternal. Dowden's demand that the activity of the conscious faculty is as necessary to perceive Good as the unconscious is the basis of his dissension with Matthew Arnold. Arnold held to "a stream of tendency not ourselves making for righteousness," a *reductio ad absurdum* to Dowden, who insisted that the stream of tendency be a conscious will, though not to the exclusion of the unconscious: "And for my part I don't know what such a stream of tendency can be, knowing nothing which cognizes righteousness, except a *person*—a conscious will; nor am I metaphysical enough to find the conception of God as a person (*person including the unconscious*—so allying itself with Pantheism—as well as the conscience; it does so in the case of ourselves) more full of difficulty for the intellect, heart, or the imagination, than that of a 'stream of tendency'. . . ." [44] In other words, the Good, apprehended by the unconscious, intuitive faculty is realized only by the conscious will, by the conscious and the unconscious energies interpenetrating one another.

More frequently, the time-eternity dialectic appears in Dowden's discussion of death and immortality. Immortality is not something by which mortality shall be swallowed up, as classical Christianity would affirm (1 Corinthians 15); it is, indeed, a description of existence. The good which exists now, Dowden declares, must persist through the unknown change men call death. Immortality thus becomes an attribute of mortality. The individual as a part of the whole cannot be lost because he is "a spiritual atom and indivisible"; and, though mortal, he is also immortal.[45]

VI   *The Imagination as the Bond*

The fourth basic tenet of Transcendentalism noticeable in Dowden's works is the imagination as the catalytic agent that brings about the coalescence of the conscious and the unconscious energies; it is the agent which effects the union between the ideal and the real or actual, the link between "the intellectual conception and the visible fact," the unifying power which brings together two apparently antagonistic elements—the testimony of the senses and its correction by the intellect. To apply to Dowden

what he said of Wordsworth's conception of the imagination, it is the "instrument for discovery of truth" that will pierce through the accidental circumstances of the situation to point out the divine reality which they conceal. Never at variance with the full and complete perception of fact, the imagination links the two worlds of the conscious and the unconscious; but it also partakes of both. It belongs at once to the world of the spontaneous instincts and to that of the self-conscious intellect and yet "travels to and fro between" the two. On one side, imagination is faith, belief, passion, intuition, vision, "spiritual insight," "unconscious cerebration"; on the other, it is intellect, reason, will. Both sides are equally operative in apprehending reality, which is life.

At times, however, Dowden seems to trust more the unconscious, instinctive side as the source reliable for penetrating into the mysteries of life. In a letter dated 1873, he said, for instance, "I have great faith in the influence of unconscious mental operation," and a decade later he wrote: "I am not less inclined to trust the spiritual intuitions 'or grasps of guess' of our highest human souls, than I was in the earlier days." [46] "Unconscious cerebration" may bring a little light on "truth transcendental." [47] A "vague outlook on things is about the most enriching mood one can know. One becomes a part of nature, and grows." [48] He says, in a sense, that spiritual truths are spiritually discerned:

> The secret may be whispered in the shrine,
> Life's central word, or cried in all men's ears
> Down from the mountain height, it yet is mine:
> —*He only who had heard the secret hears.*[49]

These are, however, but overstatements to emphasize one part of a two-part truth; for Dowden's view asserts the need of both intuitive and conscious intellectual activity, both imagination and reason. Where there is one, there is the other; for neither denies the other: they are properly aids or adjuncts one to the other. The result of their reciprocal relationship is order and harmony: when the two are fused in one, then the "soul echoes orchestrally the orchestrations of nature and of humanity." [50] If the reciprocal relationship is broken, distortion results in both life and art.

It has been noticed thus far how the spiritual powers of nature drive man towards the material realization of ethical goals, how

man is both agent and actor in bringing these goals to pass in the
human realm, and how the imagination is that faculty in man
which has to do with the effectual union of the ideal and the actual. It has been seen that, unless man is in harmony with the
spiritual powers, unless his heart and will are "right with God and
Man," his imagination becomes "cloudy," lopsided. It has also
been observed that the imagination is the catalytic agent fusing
both instinctive, unconscious energy and intellectual, conscious
activity.

Yet to be shown, however, is Dowden's concept of love as the
most significant attribute of the link between the ideal and the
real and to demonstrate, as will be seen in Chapter Three, the
drive of the "spirit in sense" towards the material realization of
esthetic goals. The correspondence between man and that which
is outside him is brought about by a love which connects man
with his fellowman and with the things of nature. "Love and
faith," Dowden affirmed, "are pillars of the universe." "Who are
chief counsellors of me?" he asked in a poem entitled "By the
Sea";[51] "Who know my heart's desire and every secret thing?"

> Three of one fellowship: the encompassing
> Strong Sea, who mindful of Earth's ancient woe
> Still surges on with swift, undaunted flow
> That no sad shore should lack his comforting;
> And next the serene Sky, whether he ring
> With flawless blue a wilderness, or show
> Tranced in the Twilight's arms his fair child-star;
> *Third of the three, eldest and lordliest,*
> *Love,* all whose wings are wide above my head,
> Whose eyes are clearer heavens, whose lips have said
> Low words more rare than the quired sea-songs are,—
> O love, high things and stern thou counsellest. (Italics added)

The love Dowden refers to goes beyond love that attaches itself to
its object exclusive of all else. Not so limited, love as Dowden
conceives it is a spirit of life in which man moves. As he states in a
lyric "Love's Lord":

> Thou known Unknown, dark, radiant sea
> In whom we live, in whom we move,
> My spirit must lose itself in Thee
> Crying a name—Life, Light, or Love.[52]

Not contained within the limitations of the finite, "borne from the infinite," love lies beyond man's pursuit and grasp of it. Owning no allegiance to time, it never fades:

> I let my plummet sink and sink
> Into this sea of blessing; when,
> Or where should it touch shoal? I think
> Love lies beyond our furthest ken.
> "The Plummet" [53]

Like beauty and thought, love goes "down among the roots of things." This self-transcending love the Ancient Mariner felt when he blessed the water-snakes, or Coleridge when he called an ass "brother," or Dowden when he addressed a sea anemone as "my little brother, the anemone!" [54] This love is a force determining the life and development of man; it is the "white-breasted" nourisher, "queen of life." Love is the passion essential to veritable knowledge, just as knowledge and the intellect are necessary to the regulation of the passions. Knowledge uninformed by love "ever lands us in illusions . . . but the knowledge involved in love is veritable and is verified at least for us who love." [55]

Before concluding this discussion, the relationship of Dowden's viewpoint to Comtianism should be considered. Because of Dowden's own emphasis on the necessity of sympathy with concrete fact, the views of Auguste Comte at first attracted him. If Dowden had been forced to choose between Comtian Positivism and speculation, illusion, or self-projected idealism, Dowden would have preferred Positivism. But Positivism denied to human knowledge the ability to pass beyond the region of phenomena, beyond the coexistence and succession of objects of perception, to know "Cause and Substance," the "two points of brightness" which Dowden believed "were to lead us into day." [56] Hence, he could write concerning Positivism: "I would suppress real life to be a disciple of Comte"; "I shall be grieved to add a hair to the Positivist side of the balance";[57] "I have given, and am giving, the Positivist in me a fair chance, but I shall not be surprised if in the end that limber transcendentalist in me should take the other fellow by the throat and make an end of him." [58] "I confess, to *me* personality, science, the will, the sense of right and wrong, become infinitely more real and precious when I look at them as manifestations of a transcendent Unknown somewhat:—*then* one rejoices in their development as something far worthier than self-aggrandizement or the mere development of a race of ever perishing units." [59]

One may readily see how closely related to the ethical doctrines of Comte are Dowden's exaltation of humanity and his insistence on moral duty. The Heaven of the Positivist is a moral life gained through his achievements. Indeed, the ninth sacrament of Comte's religion (coming seven years after death) is the solemn incorporation with the *Grand Être* of Humanity of the dead one who had devoted his whole life to the service of Humanity. Like Comte, Dowden also spoke of noble joys attained by doing good, but there was a deeply rooted difference between their views. Comte postulated morality as the coordination of all the tendencies of human nature: the good of others is the only ultimate motivation on which men should permit themselves to act—an interpretation which Dowden believed was not in keeping with the facts of human nature. "The coordination of all the tendencies of our nature is not morality," he averred; "it is much more—spirituality." [60] The Positivists, he protested, had overlooked man's universal religious instincts, for proof of which he added an anecdote: "Byron and Coleridge were walking together. A drunken man reeled past and Byron pointed to him, with the question, 'Does that confirm your opinion of man's belief in the immortality of the soul?' 'Your question does,' said Coleridge." [61] What Dowden needed more than Positivism was "communion with God." This deeply rooted need of God, of a Power beyond himself, prohibited Dowden from becoming a disciple of Comte, whose philosophy he respected for its faithfulness to concrete fact, but which he rejected because of its denial of "Cause and Substance."

In conclusion: Dowden's dialectic is not unlike that which characterized the Transcendental philosophy of Schelling, Wordsworth, Coleridge, Maurice, and Oersted—with all of whom he himself recognized kinship of viewpoint; and frequently his views are expressed in terms at once theistic, mystical, and Christian. The comparison between the frank revelations of Dowden's thought in his personal letters and in his poetry and its more cryptic public expression in his critical essays and biographical studies has indicated that more of the public statements are explained by the private ones than the reverse. Indeed, the religious mystical approach to the understanding of the universe of the Irish critic, laid bare in the letters and poetry, is but obliquely revealed in his published essays and biographies.

CHAPTER 3

Natural Signs and Cloudy Symbols: Esthetic Theory and Its Application

> . . . art should mediate between the spiritual and the material.—*Puritan and Anglican*, p. 31.

> She knew that poetry to be of permanent value must do more than reflect a passing fashion; that in a certain sense it must in its essence be out of time and space, expressing ideas and passions which are arts of our abiding humanity."—*Robert Browning*, p. 123.

IN a time when the validity of poetic knowledge and the reality of a spiritual world were being challenged by the empirical assertions of scientific materialism, poets and critics alike sought a satisfying solution. Responses to the challenge differed radically, and writers may be divided into three groups: those who retreated from scientific empiricism to an enthusiastic confidence in the esoteric poetic vision—the mythmakers, like Blake, Shelley, and Yeats; those, on the other hand, who adjusted their art to the demands of science—the Naturalist-Realists, like Balzac and Zola; and, finally, those who endeavored to achieve a unity of opposites, not by an escape from the insistent demands of Positivism, nor by a surrender of the trustworthiness of their poetic experience, but by an acceptance of the validity of both by a dialectic which reconciled the tension between them—the "spiritualists," like Wordsworth, Goethe, and Dowden.

Before T. S. Eliot and Allen Tate, Dowden had diagnosed *la maladie du siècle*—the modern dissociation of sensibility—and had endeavored to cope with it in a dialectic that would be true to both spiritual and material worlds. Whether such a reconciliation as he attempted is possible at all remains unanswered to this day. For the following question is unanswered: is it possible to reconcile the autotelic objectivity of science, which postulates a nonspiritual universe and the sufficiency of mechanical law, with the subjectivity of Romantic idealism? Like T. S. Eliot and Allen Tate, though differing in the direction of his commitment, Dowden offered his solution in terms of a metaphysically and religiously oriented esthetic.

I *The Literary Artist and His Artistic Experience*

Because of the times, the authors of the Victorian period, including Dowden, were searching for some coherent concept of life that would bring unity to their emotions, and law and impulse to their will; they desired to see life "whole," as Matthew Arnold put it. Dowden's nature demanded such a coherent view of life; he found no joy in "chopped up facts," ones unrelated to a Wholeness of things. "One may study a tree in the form of sawdust," he stated once; "but I should rather be a titmouse hopping and chirping in its branches. . . . To me personality, science, the will, the sense of right and wrong, become infinitely more real and precious when I look at them as manifestations of a transcendent Unknown somewhat. . . . Then, too, the impersonal, the sinking back, the approaches to that Unknown are all precious—and the two movements out and in—centrifugal and centripetal—the systole and diastole—make up a pulse of life." [1]

Dowden's attempt to reconcile unity and variety in poetic experience focuses on his belief of "spirit in sense," an "illuminated realism," an art true at once to primary sensations and to creative imagination—a bold faith in an age of doubt and skepticism. But Dowden believed that "faith and creativity go hand in hand and that some of the most creative natures refuse to be limited to a demonstrable materialistic universe." [2] The penetrative vision that Dowden demands of art appears quite like the revelation of absolute truth expected of religion; "He who has Art, has also Religion," wrote Goethe; and there is a sense in which Dowden saw this view as true. "It is impossible to live art rightly," he wrote in an unpublished lecture, "without a seriousness and an exaltation of temper which is akin to the religious temper; art spiritualizes the mind or should spiritualize it when it begets admiration and love and not mere dilettante pleasure, the vanity of the connoisseur and the avarice of the collector. Art, seriously engaged in, admits one to a higher life." [3]

Essential to Dowden's literary theory, therefore, is the blending of the subjective element in perfect harmony with the outer world, the compenetration of the personal with the impersonal. When an author acts from the merely personal, Dowden believes, his work tends towards introspection and a sterile egoism. But when, on the other hand, he acts in sympathy with external nature on the basis of spiritual enlightenment, his works become creations of "the Divine Power and Beauty of which they are the off-set." [4] In an early essay, "Poetical Feeling for External Nature," external phenomena become "natural signs" whose significance, rightly apprehended by the poet, puts him in contact with natural truth:

In the simplest sense the appearances of the world around us are natural signs appealing through the senses to the heart and soul, and interpreted by the imagination. The depths and fulness of the interpretation varies according to the faculty of the interpreter, but when this is of a true kind it never operates arbitrarily. The objects and phenomena of the external world, by laws as strict and universal as any law of science, produce in us certain appropriate emotions, and in these emotions reside principles which guide (unerringly in a great poetical nature) the interpreting power of the imagination. . . . When we disregard the natural signs and the real relations between external appearances and human emotions, and when we *read into* the appearances of nature some private allegorical meanings of our own, our poetry is always bad.[5]

The senses here are declared to be supersensible, especially in the poet, who, Dowden states in his "Last Words on Shelley," "feels more exquisitely than other men, and receives more impulses and intimations from the spiritual side of things." [6] The fact of sensation is produced by a vague sympathy, itself an evidence of the living unity of all things. But sensation is always associated with perception, which is largely the work of the imagination: the eye confers as well as receives; in Dowden's analysis there is no purely sensational experience. The real fact is not a material one; observation supplies only one side of it, for reflection must supply the other.[7] Therefore, the ideas and forms of sensibility which should characterize great art arise from both the senses and the intellect.

It is to be noticed that the imagination, which Dowden understands as the mediator between sensation and perception, cooperates somewhat vaguely and mystically with what he calls "the Divine in all things," and that the imagination does not copy but creates after its model, an activity at once conscious and subconscious. When one speaks instinctively, Nature is speaking through one. What Dowden said in an unpublished lecture on Ralph Waldo Emerson about the dominant idea of this philosopher may be said of his own view: "Each man may find within him, if he will but seek, something more than what is merely personal, something impersonal and universal, the divine impulse and the divine law and that this is indeed the very root of his being. Deep in the consciousness of every man he may find the meeting point between the individual will and the universal law; there is the quickest point of personality . . . yet which transcends our personality."

Most truly pursued, art is life emergent, which is described variously by Dowden as the "flow of reality and living truth," as the growth of a flower, as a "revelation" of the mysteries of existence, as "sunlight" working in a "silent, spiritual way," or as the "winds blowing where they list." Art is both "life" and the "outcome of life," both infinite and finite, at one and the same time the product of man and the product of Nature, the interpenetration of the conscious and the unconscious forces of life.[8] Artistic creativity, as Dowden understands it, is strikingly analogous to the budding and blossoming of the flower as portrayed in one of his poems, "Bud and Blossom"; both are *life* manifesting itself:

> O sweet and blind commotion of the sap
> When the first ray thrills in the folded flower!
> Virginal rapture tremulous; some great hap
> Befallen; a law declared; a quickening power.
>
> And henceforth life shall surely have a part
> In all that joy which makes the many One,
> The petals sever; the whole scented heart
> Lies naked for encounter with the sun.[9]

Because the artist cooperates in the highest sense with life as it is, "the one life within and abroad" as Coleridge stated it, his work may be considered as a purveyor of truth, beauty, and goodness. In Dowden's theory, it is impossible to separate esthetics from ethics and religion. In commenting on some of his own poetic attempts, he stated: "What is just and true and beautiful is so little personal, gets . . . away from the individual and into nature that one cannot be *praised* for it." [10]

The end and aim of art to Dowden is the manifestation and the enjoyment of beauty. Art is an embodiment of beauty, and the beautiful is a perfect experience of nature. For Dowden, as for Edmund Spenser, beauty is twofold, sensual and material, elevating and spiritual:

There is beauty which is a mere pasture for the eye; it is a spoil for which we grow greedy; as we gaze on it we sink in waves of deep delight; it leaves us faint with too much luxury of heart. And there is the higher beauty of which the peculiar quality is a penetrating radiance; it illumines all that comes into its presence; it is a beam from the Divine Fount of Light; it lifts up the soul of man out of the mire of this world; it pierces him with a sacred joy; it animates him to pure and passionate endeavor.

To Spenser and to Wordsworth it could not seem desirable to put out the right eye, because to both the eye was an inlet of divine things for the uses of the spirit. With respect to beauty, Spenser's teaching is that true beauty is always sacred, always ennobling to the spirit which is itself sane and pure, but the sensual mind will put even beauty to sensual uses. And he declares further that there is a forged or feigned beauty, which is no more than a fair illusion covering inward foulness and shame. The true beauty, according to Spenser, may be recognized by a certain illuminating quality; it is not mere pasture of the eye; rather it smites the gazer, long accustomed to the dimness of common things, as if with sudden and exquisite light; it is indeed a ray derived from God, the central Luminary of the universe.[11]

What Dowden says of Spenser in the first paragraph and of both Spenser and Wordsworth in the second is true also of his own view. The eye which functions as an inlet for divine things sees spiritual beauty in material beauty: an insight which leaves small play for the merely sensuous, for not only does it enlighten, but it also quickens and motivates to joy and participation. Such insight not only makes man aware of ideal beauty but empowers him to move towards its actualization in life; and its material representation comes about in art, the best expression of faith in spiritual beauty—art in all of its forms: painting, sculpture, literature, and music.

William Blake's and Michelangelo's art, for example, lighten "the veil that lies between men and the Spiritual Unknown"; and Turner's pictures are "not views but essences." [12] Poetry, too, reveals the beauty of the world, Dowden asserts in a poem entitled "Poesia": it shows both the finite and infinite beauty of the world, and the poem is itself a part of that beauty. Poetry is both revealer of beauty and beauty revealed. As revealer of beauty, poetry partakes of the finite: "Plant firm on Earth her feet"; "She needs be no more pure than a dove is." As beauty revealed, poetry partakes of the infinite: "Her sacred vesture must elude all mortal touch"; and as such, it is "no more to be possessed than sunsets are."

Because Dowden believes art to be informed with the good and true and beautiful, he talks of it as a didactic influence—but not as didactic in the sense of directly or indirectly teaching or inculcating moral truth; instead, art presents a direct vision of human life in which one does not seek truth and beauty but is enveloped by them.[13] In this sense Dowden speaks of the function of art as being to "exercise and invigorate the soul," and of the poet as "a moral pioneer." Shakespeare, for example, did not indoctrinate but furnished men with "the power to free, arouse, dilate"; and his creation of Cordelia in particular strengthened men's faith in mankind and enriched the tradition of human goodness. Shelley through his poetry also enabled men to conceive more nobly of nature and of man. In this sense Spenser and Wordsworth are "teachers"; and Goethe, also, is useful for the illumination and enrichment of life. In fact, only that artist who has in some way enriched human life and enabled men to become better or less incomplete can be called "great." And in the measure that the artist reveals truth, he is a "prophet" or "priest." Just as Dowden required the artist to be morally faithful in his presentation of experience, so did he require the critic directly or indirectly to enrich life.

Dowden's "two movements out and in—centrifugal and centripetal—the systole and diastole" not only "make up a pulse of life" but also describe the process of creation of great literature. Artistic activity is the manner in which the artist acquires disinterestedness, the anonymity essential to great art, at the same time that he retains the uniqueness of his expression, the lyric intensity of his genius. In artistic activity, that which exists outside the artist and apart from him and that which the mind of the artist discovers as the interpretation of the object must fuse so that matter and form become "one illuminated reality." The poet needs to move out in the observation of concrete life, return to inspire his garnered wisdom with poetic feeling, and then, by aid of the imagination, restore it to the world in a finer form. Dowden's view of the creativity of the imagination is, therefore, much like Coleridge's concept of the Secondary Imagination.

For Coleridge, the Secondary Imagination reworks the sensory material apprehended perceptually into concrete symbols of the self, the absolute, the world, and God, which otherwise are apprehended conceptually by the Reason. Dipping into concrete facts provides the steadying and the restraint that the emotions of the poet need and saves him from the arrogance and extravagance of the completely personal element. While the poet seems thus to lose himself, he finds himself paradoxically through sympathy with external nature: "The shallow . . . consider liberty a release from all law, from every constraint. The wise see in it, on the contrary, the potent Law of Laws, namely, the fusion and combination of the conscious will, or partial individual law, with those universal, eternal, unconscious, which run through all Time, pervade history, prove immortality, give moral purpose to the entire objective world, and the last dignity to human life." [14] These statements reveal the basic belief in an organic unity of all things, one in which both activity and passivity are essential to the poet's experience and in which both Nature and the poet contribute in the creation of the artifact: "The joy of quick-stirring senses is met as it were by a kindred joy in the stream that sparkles, and the fish that leaps, and the wind that sings, and the clouds that fly." [15] The relation between the outer and the inner worlds of the poet should be a vital flow from the mythic, inner significance to its outer historical perception, and vice versa.

II   Hazards of Creativity

Artistic creativity as Dowden describes it defends the artist against two dangers threatening his work: (1) concentration on independent and isolated abstractions and (2) absorption by impersonal concretions; for neither should ever gain victory. Though Dowden does not define abstraction, he contrasts "the abstraction of thought" with "the visionary power of imagination" in favor of the latter. From Dowden's paraphrases and appositives one comprehends that the word "abstract" and its cognates refer to that activity of the mind which creates independently of the information conveyed by the senses and which is confirmed by a universal consensus. It is within the power of the artist to withdraw himself from the influence and restraint of historical or local patterns of life and to project an independent and isolated mythology in harmony with his peculiar genius. His withdrawal on behalf of freedom may take several forms—desertion of tradition, projection of fantasies, or creation of lifeless symbols. The visionary power of imagination, on the other hand, immerses its vision in the historical and concrete patterns of life.

The artist, in order to save himself from the hazards inherent in personal vision, should interrelate with "human tradition ever growing and shaping our lives"; for there is nothing individual in beauty. The harmonious interaction of the individual intellect with history and tradition leads to the discovery of beauty, and artists who despise tradition and would discard it as a useless crutch are precisely those who fail in their quest. Instead of seeking for truth with both the eye and the imagination, they pursue their own dreams and desires; they imaginatively project their own color and form upon ideas and distort all relation to external reality. In Dowden's scheme of things, it is a foolish notion of the artist to insist on his freedom and right to a personal vision and to ignore tradition, for a precondition of his freedom is life in society. Since reality is an organic whole of interrelated parts, the artist who thus isolates himself can have no thoughts of a real world and, therefore, no consciousness of freedom. His insistence on a purely private vision effects a tourniquet dilemma, an injury and a loss both to himself and to society.

What Dowden means by tradition is curiously complex: it is colored by religious and by cultural, historical, and social concerns; and, in general, it is all that the Western world in the nineteenth century had inherited from preceding generations. Bequests of preceding generations that were distinctive to his times, the ideas with which he is chiefly concerned, were a belief in evolution and human progress, the scientific spirit and the consequent divorce of imagination and reason, and the concept of democracy. Other bequests, common to men of his day as well as to preceding generations, were the knowledge that man is, and has been throughout all recorded history, less than perfect; that man has a mythical, religious, or philosophical bent which craves information beyond what is observable and verifiable; and that all human knowledge is relative.

Dowden assumes these beliefs, as facts of existence in the nineteenth century necessary to be acknowledged by any writer and integrated in his work. As a poet and critic, what he ultimately wanted was to find subject matter—general myth—common to the nineteenth-century writer and to his audience. While he required writers to respect their traditional inheritance and to build on its contribution of wisdom and prudence, he denied to them the possibility of reviving past cultures. The advancement of knowledge and of spiritual insights enlightened modern man in his upward progress towards truth irretrievably beyond his predecessors.

Early in Dowden's career in a lecture on Goethe, he grappled with another aspect of the problem of the possible isolation of the artist from society: may a man devote himself and his time wholly to the study and creation of Beauty? What position should the culture of the faculties which apprehended the Beautiful hold in the life of the man? Should anything in a man's life, either work or leisure or happiness, be cultivated at the expense of another part of his nature? Based on the belief that no part of a man's nature can be beneficially developed while any part remains separated, Dowden's answer was an emphatic "No." His answer is comparable to Matthew Arnold's, probably even influenced by it; for both critics believed that exclusive development of one part of a man's nature at the expense of another resulted in practical evil. The artist who locks himself in his ivory tower exposes himself to the danger of "nourishing the fancy in solitude." As a counterpoise, he needs to lay hold of the real world by engaging in public activities.

An example of a poet who disciplined himself by engagement in public affairs was Goethe, for he spent his years in Weimar largely in superintendence of state affairs, the working of mines, and the marshalling of troops. Because his occupation with public affairs during this time forced him to turn outward, much of "the mists of youthful passion and sentiment" cleared away. All the later lyrical poems of Goethe of that period disclose an increasing objective tendency, a deliberate involvement of the imagination with reality, "until both beat to one tune and time, and the secret of the life of things became his." [16]

Not all critics, however, have interpreted as Dowden did the change in Goethe's outlook which began to occur in Weimar, for some described his scientific pursuits as a marked decline of his poetic temperament. Dowden, on the contrary, interpreted the change as "a clarifying of his first fervours, a consolidating of his scattered powers, an earnest marshalling of all the powers of his being for something better than a vague outcry of enthusiasm or a wail of melancholy egoism, a marshalling of his powers for definite, positive achievement." [17] He felt it important to insist that Goethe the poet and the man of science were not at odds: "they held hands, and each spoke inspiring words to the other." [18]

With the aim of seeing things as they are even more clearly, Goethe journeyed into Italy. He wanted to tune his soul to the very givenness of things, "to accept them with a clear and loving eye, to renounce all pretensions, to seek neither after originality or ingenuity nor a clever phrase." His entrance into Italy some critics have spoken of as a new birth, as a salvatory experience that made Goethe a new man; but Dowden felt it to be little more than a sudden expansion of a movement already begun in Weimar. Goethe's life as a statesman in Weimar, together with his studies in physical science, had also involved him in the objective world. He was not concentrating on his own emotions at that time but was embracing the outer world of men and things. The two opposing tendencies in Goethe—subjective and objective, personal and impersonal, unity and variety—met and were reconciled; and these tendencies for the sake of clarification of his view, Dowden called "the man from under the sign of the microcosm and the man from under the sign of the macrocosm":

Conceive to yourselves two opposite types of men—one, who finds his be-all and end-all within the narrow compass of *his* own breast—narrow, and yet infinite in desires, in aspirations, in striving, towards thoughts beyond the reaches of our souls, who broods upon his own passion, who is therefore weak and restless, with no clear outlook on the external world; who is therefore suspicious of his fellows; yet who thrills to the touch of love, a man of genius, a Werther, perhaps a

Hamlet. Consider such a type of man, and now consider his opposite; one who has subdued his self-will, his turbulent desires, his dreams, his extravagant thoughts, who turns his eye outward on the large, substantial world, who binds his life to the life of his fellows by social action, who is therefore strong, calm, prudent, who masks his face under forms and delays, and compromises and courtesies; no man of genius perhaps; at least not offering his genius as a sacrifice on the altar to be lit by heavenly fire; but one who is a master of the machinery of life; who can deal with the world with calmly energetic, shaping hands. It is a mistake to name one of these men the poet, and the other the statesman or to name one the dreamer and the other the man of actions. The contrast between them is wider and deeper than these names suggest. I will call them *the man born under the sign of the microcosm; and the man born under the sign of the macrocosm.* There are no other titles so fitting.

Now in Goethe these two men existed side by side. . . . In the early Weimar period these two personalities appear playing their parts. The man of the microcosm was being trained and taught by the noble soul of Frau von Stein, the man of the macrocosm was superintending mines, raising recruits, regulating finances for Karl August. Which of the two was to be the master? Or was it possible that they might some happy day hold hands in a mutually beneficent friendship? . . . In *Tasso* . . . Antonio . . . is at Tasso's side; he takes him by the hand. The man of the macrocosm and the man of the microcosm have met, and are reconciled; genius stands supported by intelligence and will. . . . Italy was the genius which placed for Goethe the hand of the Tasso within him in that of the Antonio. Henceforth rivalry ceased; friendship between the two was sealed.[19]

The struggle between the claims of idealism and realism in Goethe is the struggle, in one or another aspect, which becomes the general theme of his works. *Werther* demonstrates "the ruin that comes upon a pure idealist" who will not and cannot abandon his dreams and immoderate desires. *Tasso* exemplifies how a "triumphant worldliness comes to deliver the idealist when he cannot deliver himself." [20] *Wilhelm Meister* and its companion work *Faust* study the conflict: one queries what can be accomplished by conscious self-direction and education; the other studies what may be done for man by the whole of existence. Wilhelm Meister, a foolish idealist, needed to be rescued from the prison of his idle dreams and to be rehabilitated to a real life of modest well-doing. Faust, too, originally conceived as an idealist, needed to be turned from "his own private thoughts and dreams to the real world."

Mephistopheles, the cynical spirit in Faust, the realist in him, will seduce Faust, if possible, into seeing only the mean side of reality and into accepting it apart from that idealistic, elevating spirit which ennobles man's activity; he is the cynical ego of Faust which questions whether the union of the poetic subjective and the prosaic objective represents a true possibility in human life.

The conflict between idealism and realism within the artist does not always end, however, in a compromise as felicitous as Goethe's. Some artists in their desire to be original deny or desert tradition. Blake molded the world to resemble himself, and he looked on nature to see through it; and, in so doing, he indulged in the illusory and egoistic. The facts of the world glided away from him and were replaced by ideas. The portrait painted in his works was not of life as it is—both subjective and objective—but of "naked primal truths," "cloudy symbols of some high spiritual romance." [21] Only if Blake had recognized his roots in the universal spirit in all things, real as well as ideal, could he have delivered himself from such a fragmentary and isolated vision, says Dowden, or from an art that is, therefore, unreal.

Characters created by Blake and by artists like him tend to become abstractions; they are bloodless creatures only partially related to real men and women and to their experiences in life. In creating characters, such artists start from an abstraction which they clothe with humanity and concrete form; or, conversely, they seek to type the individual according to one prominent trait and ignore those characteristics special to him. Such typical or representative characters are nothing but "personified opinions" of the author, a hazard which Dowden would have the author avoid. "The dullest portions of Spenser's poem," for instance, "are those in which he works with most self-consciousness, piecing together definite meanings to definite symbols." [22] The better way is partly designed and deliberate, partly unconscious, coming into existence with or without the poet's awareness and almost always with implications which reach beyond his conscious thought.

Shakespeare, as an exemplary model, started with the concrete, real world, with characters and actions. He did not create his characters *ex nihilo*, nor did he make them embodied types of the passions; rather, he created from the matter of real experience: men and women living with and responding to each other in situational conflict and change. The subject of the *Merchant of Venice* is not, for example, the abstraction *revenge;* "Antonio and Shylock, Portia and Nerissa, Lorenzo and Jessica, Bassanio and Gratiano—these, and a passage in the lives of these, are the true subjects." Nor is the subject of *Romeo and Juliet* the abstraction *love,* but two young and loving hearts surrounded by a group of living figures. Shakespeare, who sought to see things as they are rather than to refine facts away into abstractions, kept his feelings and ideas well informed by concrete matter in order that, by coming into more fruitful relation with fact, they might be vitalized. As a result, he embodied the ideal in the real; for the existence of human ideals proves that this earth is not simply material. The love of Romeo and Juliet, for example, though moving on the plane of everyday experience, proves by its heroic sacrifice an ideal "that this earth of ours is not wholly a market or a counting-house." [23]

From abstractions it is easy for the idealist to pass on to lifeless symbols: "if once we leave the surface of this dear old mother-earth, we are but too likely to wander farther and farther towards the Inane." [24] In such lifeless symbolism Dowden feels that Goethe sometimes indulged because he was misled at times by a too-intensive scientific study; yet, even though tending to excess, his careful observation of natural phenomena enabled him to keep in close contact with reality. In Dowden's analysis, the symbolist fails to integrate the images of the world of sense and feeling with the world of idea and spirit; in the symbolist's pursuit of essence, the image is ignored, hence, the solipsistic nature of his art. The images of the world of sense and feeling should be integrated by the imagination with the world of idea and spirit, the resultant symbol dependent on neither one alone but on both in simultaneity. If "a natural action means something larger," then "symbolism is acceptable"; if, on the other hand, symbolism "denaturalizes action and justifies this by the larger meanings, it is bad art." [25]

For the method of the scientist in discovering truth is not essentially different from that of the poet, Dowden reasoned in an early letter of February, 1873: in the totality of human nature there is "something truth-discovering at work" by which even scientific discoveries are made, an imaginative vision, a moment of faith when a man is "most truly in harmony with the facts outside [himself]" and more in contact with reality.[26] But the least over-confidence in a private vision and any departure from the general myth which regulates that vision leads the wanderer to inane symbolism and "puerile utopias." For the real world is the starting point of all creative activity for Dowden, the real world which includes natural objects and the varied experiences of man; and matter from the real world becomes in the artifact the "natural signs" or symbols.

Equally as hazardous to the creation of great art as the artist's concentration on independent and isolated abstractions is a second hazard of creativity: the possibility of his absorption by impersonal concretions. Just as the artist may wrap himself in an unreal world of ideas so that the external world may seem no longer to exist in relation to him, so may he lose the uniqueness of his personal vision by total surrender to externality. The impersonal detachment that he seeks in the concrete facts of life to strengthen and control his vision may become an anarchic chaos of details threatening alike his individual view and the unity of his art. In the event of such absorption, the artist is reduced to a part of nature; his independence and originality are minimized, and he himself is resolved "into the resultant of environing forces," "the natural and inevitable product of ancestry and ambient circumstances." Because he becomes lost in the details which should have saved his art, the artifact he produces becomes merely "an accumulation of ingenious observations, not a work of art"; ". . . his art suffers by his inability to lay some of his gatherings of facts aside." [27] Dowden recognizes, therefore, the power of environment to form the artist and to determine his action; but he does not do so to the exclusion of a similar recognition of the artist's freedom of will. To deny to the artist his plastic power, he believed, would be to deny freedom to man in general. One notices that Dowden's esthetics is rooted deeply, as ever, in his metaphysics.

The preoccupation of the late nineteenth century with scientific realism left little room for the exercise of imagination. External nature became merely a collection of objects, subject to certain general laws which may be described in detail. The faithful observation of the nature of men and things called for by the disinterestedness of scientific realism threatened to overweigh the artist's imagination and to make his art little more than a mirror of life as it is. Such verisimilitude, Dowden judged, would destroy the unity of art just as surely as abstractions threatened it. On these grounds he severely criticized the Realists, such as Zola and Balzac, as incapable of making art from observation alone.

Dowden's radical rejection of the Realists leads one to ask what he meant by the "illuminated realism" to which he insisted that art be faithful. Foremost in his concept of realism is his theory of history, one basically optimistic in its evaluation of the past and present and in its prevision of the future, a view which regards men as progressing ever upward towards a better and more complete humanity. If this evolution or progress is so, must the "old arts" and "old types of beauty" be cast aside for the newer forms? "Well, be it so," he replies; "let us bid them a cheerful farewell, and confidently expect some new and as yet inconceivable manifestations of the spirit of order and beauty which can never become extinct while man remains man." [28] In a poem called "Inner Life," one finds the idea similarly expressed: "What boots it to look back? The world is ours, / Come, we will fare, my brother, boldly forth; / Let that dread Angel wave the sword of flame / Forever round relinquished bowers— / Leave Eden there; we will subdue the earth." [29]

In an unpublished lecture about Bunyan, Dowden contends that one cannot expect to find in oneself precisely the same forms of feeling as those which had characterized a preceding generation. To attempt to revive "the exact mode of thought and feeling of the seventeenth century," for instance, would be "insanity." The external conditions change from age to age, and man's conquest of the difficulties besetting him will differ, at least in details, from that of his predecessors. The essential truths, however, abide from one generation to another. In the case of the seventeenth century, the truths essential to Puritanism in general, as urgent to modern man as to the seventeenth-century Puritan, remain—"its seriousness, its ardour, its plea for the loins girt and the lamp lit." In particular, Bunyan's religious history as recorded in *Grace Abounding*, Dowden claims, "may be repeated in every age in its essentials, for it is the history of a soul struggling from darkness to light, from confusion to clearness, from self-division to unity." [30]

The great artist, as Dowden conceived him, is a pioneer; he is ever pushing towards new frontiers of the good, beautiful, and true. If he should seek repose in the midst of the temporal flux of things, his art must be judged as false to the living unity of nature. Rossetti's marriage poems, Dowden avers, falsely represent love because the poet celebrates a static attainment with a worship of bodily grace and charm. He fails to represent the common reality of high love, which is not a static attainment but that "ardent tending towards worthy ends with interchange of perfect service." [31] Attainment or fulfillment which Rossetti saw as the permanent condition is to be found in the midst of the striving—or nowhere at all according to Dowden. Clearly, in Dowden's view of the truth, which is the concern of art, there can be no separation, as has already been indicated, between that which becomes and that which is. Hence, art must confront all new contributions of knowledge in the hope that, from the confrontation of the imagination with newly gained insight, some higher and previously unimagined forms of beauty might arise.

Obviously, Dowden's linear view of history differentiates his realism from the patterns of the ordinary Realist whose art represents an imitative response to the outer world, a copy-objectivity. Imitation is essential to both realisms, to be sure, and to the somewhat passive reception of data as well; but, for Dowden, the outer world of phenomena and the inner world of the artist cooperate somewhat mystically in producing the highest art. Correlated with the sensory data of the outer world is "an ideal element, an invisible element which unites itself to our perceptions, and while the element which may be called the material one remains constant, this ideal element is subject to continual variation and development." [32] Thus, the artist, as a midwife working with nature, delivers the artifact which both have produced.

As for how the imagination may use scientific knowledge for the purposes of art, Dowden lists, in his essay "The Scientific Movement and Literature" (1887), the four ideas of modern science which have value for the imagination: "First, the vastness of the universe, and of the agencies at work in it; secondly, the idea of law; thirdly, the idea of ensemble; last, the ultimate of known ultimates is *force*." Since "not the details of the specialist, but large *vues d'ensemble*" are "fruitful for the feelings and imagination of men," the idea of vastness liberates and expands the imagination of the artist from a myopic concentration with the Me (the Self) to the infinite variety of the Not-Me (otherness). The second idea, that of universal law, brings order out of the endless variety and the infinite complexity that characterize the vastness of the universe. Dowden subdivides universal law into two kinds—

physical and moral—and in doing so reveals his departure from the strict materialistic conception of the universe. In 1873 he wrote to Miss West: "Of late my attitude has been this—that the materialistic construing of the facts of the world, is after all only a construing—not an experience at all—that a different construing is altogether as possible. . . . In fact, after a materialistic period I am almost sure that the difficulties of materialism will be felt very strongly and that men will return to the other hypothesis in some new forms as the less difficult of the two." [33]

The third idea, *vues d'ensemble,* corresponds with the same consensus which the artist intuitively feels to be inherent in the nature of things: "And what is the poet's confession? That the life of the least blossom in the most barren crevice is a portion of the great totality of being, that its roots are intertangled with the roots of humanity, that to give a full account of it would require a complete science of man, and a complete theology." [34] The fourth and last idea of science which the imagination may appropriate is *force,* the "ultimate datum of consciousness." Force, in Dowden's explanation, becomes somewhat of a *tertium quid,* neither subject nor object, but inherent in each one, and yet beyond both, equivalent to a supernatural Power, or to what is commonly called God. "What is this," Dowden concludes, "but an assertion, justified by the most careful analysis, that the highest truth of science and the highest truth of religion are one, and are both found in the confession of an inscrutable Power manifested to us through all external phenomena, and through our own intellect, affections, conscience, and will?" [35] The gist of the argument here is directed towards reinstating religious and poetic knowledge as truth-bearers that are as respectable as the scientific knowledge that first rendered them suspect. And how better can this reinstatement be accomplished than by making religious and poetic knowledge aspects of scientific knowledge? By such persuasion Dowden attempts to make whole once again the dissociated sensibility of modern man.

Insensibility on the part of the artist to the contemporary movement of science Dowden condemned, therefore, as "essentially unliterary." Especially to the reason and its dedication to exact methods of thought should the artist be sensitive; for the creative work of imagination arises from a basis of adequate knowledge and exact perception. For the reason acts upon the imagination both as its impulse and its law; it stimulates at the same time that it regulates. Reason, interacting with the imagination to create, prevents art from becoming merely sensory pleasure or dilettante's indulgence. Though the knowledge provided by the reason and though the imaginative response by the feelings are recognizably not identical, insight and knowledge yet control the feelings; and Dowden continues, "Whatever modifies our intellectual conceptions powerfully, in due time affects art powerfully." [36] Therefore, faithful to the contributions of the reason, the artist should mirror in his works "the life, the thoughts, and passions of the nations." [37] The artist who fails to do so is "not of first-rate importance" with reference to his era.

Measured by this standard James Russell Lowell, Washington Irving, and Henry Wadsworth Longfellow find a place on Dowden's index of failures. Longfellow's works generally, as an example, did not reflect American life as it was: *"Hiawatha* might have been dreamed in Kensington by a London man of letters who possessed a graceful idealizing turn of imagination . . . *Evangeline* is an European idyl of American life." [38] Nor had an accurate presentation of the American people as they were in his day captured and directed Longfellow's imagination. Even Whitman, so greatly admired by Dowden, is charged in an unpublished notebook with wronging "his naturalism" by not representing certain facts as being as "nasty, unpleasant, and disgusting" as they in reality are. By "transcending the senses in his mystical flights," Whitman denied and insulted them. "The coarse, the ugly, the terrible—Evil" are also necessary, Dowden states, to "our perception of highest beauty and greatness." [39] In fact, as it has already been observed, the inveterately optimistic Dowden could find even "on a hopeless day . . . the soul of goodness in things evil." [40] However, to concentrate too exclusively and persistently on the evil and the baser side of life was, he believed, as erroneous as to slight it.

Crucial to Dowden's view is the sacramental significance which he attaches to the facts of the world, for it was his way of bridging the gap between material and spiritual, grace and nature, body and soul, subject and object, ideal and real, science and poetry— and the pairings could continue. The "facts of religion," he proclaims, are "really as real as those of commerce or art." [41] Hence, "a faithful presentation of the world does not leave us indifferent to good and evil, but rather rouses within us, more than all maxims and all preaching can, an inextinguishable loyalty to good. It is any falsifying of those facts, whether the falsification be that of the sensualist or of the purist, whether it be a lie told to seduce us to vice, or to bribe us to virtue,—it is this which may possibly lead us aside from directness, simplicity, and uprightness of action." [42]

Dowden assumes that others are as capable as he of seeing religious significance in phenomena: as a result, he viewed Voltaire's "blindness" to such meaning as "a grave defect." Dowden expects all artists, therefore, to give the spiritual meaning of the facts of which they write—a meaning inherent in the facts themselves, so he says, and not imposed upon them. In *Shakspere: A Critical Study of His Mind and Art,* he asks the question, "Is the Elizabethan drama religious?"; and he answers "Yes" assuredly, "if the facts of the world be themselves sacred,—parts of a divine order of things, and interpenetrated by that Supreme Reality, apprehended yet unknowable, of which the world of matter and of mind are a manifestation." Moreover, Dowden would go beyond the early Wordsworth in discovering spiritual significance in things of sense; he would discover "spirit in sense" not only in hills, sky, stream, and the experience of men, but also in art forms —the "shaping of a vase, the lines and colors of a tapestry, the carving of a capital, the movement of a celebrant in the rites of religion, in a relief of Della Robbia, in a Venus of Botticelli, in the mysterious Gioconda of Leonardo." And he asks, "Why not vivify all amidst which we live and move by translating sense into spirit, and spirit into sense . . . ?" [43]

As it has been noted thus far, in Dowden's understanding, the science and the realism from which the artist is to draw his materials involve more than a materialistic conception of the universe; knowledge of religious phenomena is as scientific as that of physical; the concrete facts of life are illumined by an interpenetrating Spirit; and art's receptivity of or deviation from this view of things determines ultimately its excellence or deficiency. However, another aspect of science in relation to art concerns Dowden. With the decline of a universal myth in the nineteenth century which could provide art with subject matter common to both the artist and his audience, some artists began to emphasize, like scientists, the technical and mechanical aspects of their work—the "art-for-art's-sake" advocates. This school insisted that art embodies its own justification apart from moral content and its emphasis was placed, therefore, on "ingenuities and technical formalities." Dowden believed this emphasis was misplaced. Yet the artist was not to undervalue form and technique. Indeed, anyone who ignores form is not an artist at all; in fact, the artist who refuses to labor as a master of technique is to be censured. But, if he concentrates on form exclusive of matter, he has "divorced himself from the spiritual world, and in the midst of a material world has given himself up to low aims of self-interest;[44] and, no matter "in however exquisite little phials it may be presented, such art as he then produces is art in its "decline":

It no longer sways or controls our being; it painfully seeks to titillate a special sense. An indifference arises as to what is called the substance or "content" of works of art, and the form is spoken of as if that had a separate and independent existence. There follows . . . "the inevitable triumph of mediocrities"; executive or technical skill, of the kind which commands admiration in a period devoid of noble motives and large ideas, being attainable by persons of mere talent. The artificial refinements of a coterie are held to constitute the beautiful in art, and these can be endlessly repeated.[45]

And whatever freedom the artist has won by his novel techniques is lost when he becomes subject to them: "Even in the interest of form it is needful that a higher and finer type of beauty should be born from art than that which is attained by skilful juggling with phrases and ingenious manipulation of rhymes." [46] That is, if form is associated in an integral fashion with matter, the art it creates is an embodiment of spiritual beauty which is the end and aim of art.

Dowden's mystical affinities get the better of him here, for his position is far from clear. He states that "such an apparently mechanical thing as the stopping of a passage of verse is not mechanical, but in its essence spiritual." [47] The symmetrical arrangement of characters in Shakespeare's early plays he criticizes as "too geometrical," "artificial, not organic and vital"; Shakespeare relied too heavily on "a system of mechanism to support the structure," more on "the disposition of parts" than "the inspiration of a common life." But the interplay between the academic rules of art and *life* —as charged with philosophical implications as that word is in Dowden's literary mystique—how does it come about? Nowhere does Dowden state the relationship clearly. The brief description that he does give could just as well belong to the inspiration of a prophet as of an artist:

The growth of Shakspere's freedom, as an artist, was really identical with his passing under the influence of a higher law. . . . At first when we resolve to live a life somewhat higher than the common life of vulgar incident, we at first do well to put ourselves under a system of rules and precepts; through strict observance of these we shall secure in a certain degree the ideality our life has need of. But in due time we fling away our manuals, our codes of spiritual drill, our little rules and restrictions. A deeper order takes authority over our being, and resumes in itself the narrower order; the rhythm of our life acquires a larger harmony, a movement free and yet sure as that of nature. This is the explanation of the early manner of all great writers of verse, all great painters, and musicians, as compared with their later manner. Their style becomes free and daring because the facts of the world have now taken hold of them, and because their subjection to highest law is at length complete. They and their work are as free as the winds, or as the growing grass, or as the waves, or the drift of clouds, or the motion of the stars. As free; that is to say in complete, noble, and glad subjection.[48]

Dowden thinks of the structure, organization, versification of great art—the "system of mechanism"—as somehow endowed with the freedom of life itself, for the quantitative distinctives of the artifact are mysteriously informed with the qualitative features of life. Art, he says, is not constructed like a building by certain specifications on a blueprint, each part carefully put into its proper place; it is inspired (in the etymological sense of "breathed into") by the essence of life. In Dowden's thought, art is as much the product of intuition and inspiration as of self-conscious contrivance.

Dowden anticipated a time that would be "more favorable to true art than the present . . . when thought will be obscurely present in instinctive action, and in human emotion, and will vitalize and inspire these joyously rather than tyrannically dominate them." [49] His hopes were directed towards a harmonious unity of the two polaric tendencies of reason and imagination. To live solely on the "outskirts" of the soul "where acquisitions of knowledge are to be made" is one extreme; to depart from the concrete facts of life and live too much on the "other side of the soul (where God is)" as a kind of *"Heimweh,"* a homesickness, is the other extreme. To pursue either source of knowledge exclusively, how-ever, would constitute only a part-truth. Neither an exclusive em-phasis on scientific Realism nor on Romanticism was adequate to the demands of the totality of human nature. Realism erred by studying too persistently and exclusively the baser facts of life; Romanticism went astray by caring little for the life of the world at large. Dowden dared to hope for some *"Versöhnung"* of the antagonism between the two, for "some reconciliation nobler than any yet attained." "After the harassing search for truth and all the cross half-lights, if poetry were (not in a cowardly spirit but through zeal and deep interest in human passion and action) to occupy itself with these in a dramatic way, possibly it might re-turn to the search for truth transcendental, and find that a little light had come in the meantime." [50]

In conclusion, an overemphasis on personal vision or an exclu-sive concentration on concrete facts, either a too-idealistic or a too-realistic approach, each leads the artist to extravagance—and ul-timately to the abstraction he was trying to avoid. Only in the balanced interplay of the two can art be rescued from abstraction and find the unity between the inner conscious world and the outer unconscious that it hopes to achieve. Mills, railways, and machinery—the new things that science brought in the nineteenth century—will be integrated in new art forms "when science is learned in love, and its powers are wielded in love." For the artist not only feels an affinity with the physical order of light, motion, heat, electricity, and chemistry, but also recognizes "a moral order to which we belong, the recognition of which cannot but produce in any mind that dwells upon it an emotion which would be in-tense if it were not so massive, and of the nature of mysticism were it not in the highest degree inspired by reason." [51] With Dowden the moral is inseparably connected with the intellectual and imag-inative; he finds sanctions for the moral world both in the heart of man and through the observation of social phenomena. The art-ist's recognition of this moral order and his identification with it bring the chaotic "jumble of facts," which may threaten his work, to ultimate unity and order.

CHAPTER 4

His Struggle with Shakespeare's Positivism

> This "Study of Shakespeare" I only partly like myself, and I expect you will only partly like it. One who loves Wordsworth and Browning and Newman can never be content to wholly abandon desires and fears and affinities which are extra-mundane, even for the rich and ample life of mundane passion and action which Shakespeare reveals. This, however, is what I tried to do (and if the world and man be a manifestation of a Somewhat which lies behind them, one ought, I suppose, to be satisfied, for a time, to approach that Somewhat in this indirect way).—Dowden, *Letters*, p. 69.

I *Nature of the Conflict*

THE Shakespeare theory held by Dowden while writing his lectures in 1873 was to undergo a change in the following year: "My Shakespeare theory," he wrote, "is not quite what it was in the spring of '73, when I wrote the lectures you read. *Then* I thought he repressed his metaphysical mood and his passionate mood. *Now,* I think he adjusted the two so that neither suffered. He had his outer sphere of metaphysics and self-abandonment and *that was his truest self;* but he had his inner sphere of practicality and self-restraint." [1] Evidence of this change of interpretation appears not only in his letters but also in the publication of his revised lecture notes, *Shakspere: A Critical Study of His Mind and Art.*

The change was brought about by Dowden's reading an essay by David Masson, published in 1856, entitled "Shakespeare and

112

Goethe." Before reading Masson's essay and while writing his lectures on Shakespeare during the preceding year, Dowden had felt "a sense of repression" from Shakespeare "which was painful." After reading Masson, he attributed the sense of repression to his previously imperfect understanding of Shakespeare; he now found Shakespeare to "stimulate, urge, or impel, more than he represses." [2] Dowden therefore credited Masson with having expressed what he himself had been groping after for a year. What Masson said was that Shakespeare walked between two worlds, the finite and the infinite, and that he heartily acknowledged the concrete world and meditated ceaselessly on the spiritual. Reiteratively, Masson called attention, as Dowden did later, to Shakespeare's "concreteness as a poet," to the keenness of his attachment to all the world of the real and the concrete. But Masson also noticed that Shakespeare was also vitally concerned, but without vain speculation, with the spiritual, infinite, and unknown mystery encompassing the material, finite, and knowable.

Of Shakespeare's metaphysics, Masson wrote: "Because Shakespeare was such a votary of the concrete, because he walked so firmly on the green and solid sward of that island of life which he knew to be surrounded by a metaphysical sea, this or that metaphysical proposal with respect to the island itself occupied him but little . . . man must needs know what the island contains, and act as those who have to till and rule it; still, with that expanse of waters all round in view, and that roar of waters ever in the ear, what can men call themselves or pretend their realm to be"? [3]

Similarly, Dowden wrote that "[Shakespeare] does not, indeed, come forward with explanations of the mysteries of existence; perhaps because he felt more than other men their mysteriousness. Many of us seem to think it the all-essential thing to be provided with answers to the difficult questions which the world propounds, no matter how little the answers be to these great questions. Shakspere seems to have considered it more important to put the questions greatly, to feel the supreme problems." [4]

Thus, side by side, both the Elizabethan's positive materialism and his metaphysical restraint appear in Dowden's *Shakspere;* that is, Shakespeare presents life strictly as he sees it. The positive aspects may be explained, but the spiritual ones may defy empirical verification. A promontory into the infinite, Shakespeare,

"stretching out long and sharp, has before . . . [him] measure-
less sea and the mass of threatening cloud; behind . . . [him]
the habitable globe, illuminated, and alive with moving figures of
man and woman." [5] But such a dualism, if it actually existed in
Shakespeare as Masson affirmed it did, was contradictory to Dowden's own theory.

The discordance between Dowden's own apprehension of life
and his initial interpretation of perhaps the greatest poet troubled
Dowden. Great art, Dowden believed, as it has been previously
noticed, is an expression of *life*, which itself is best understood as
an integration of the real and the ideal, a dual unity, the finite
interpenetrated by the infinite. "Shakespeare was a discipline in
some way alien to my most vital self," he wrote in a letter on June
15, 1874; there are "certain needs not satisfied by Shakespeare."
"But, really, I think there is a deficiency in Shakespeare of recognizing the influence for good of large general ideas. Everything in
him seems to proceed from individuals." [6] Dowden's resolution of
the discordance, to state his own words, was to "put some of himself into Shakespeare in self-defense":[7] he attempted to interpret
Shakespeare's attachment to the concrete as an indirect expression
of his own affinities with Transcendental thought. Or, it could be
said, he began to mold Shakespeare's thought as Masson had elu-
cidated it into that of Goethe's. After the summer of 1874, Dowden began to interpret Shakespeare as "an idealist in thought and
in emotion, who resolves that *his idealism should be real*, and
should include, not exclude, all positive fact." [8]

II *Deletions and Additions to the Manuscript*

Significant to an understanding of Dowden's conflict with his
subject is the nature of what he deleted from his lecture manuscript on Shakespeare and what he added to it in its revision for
publication. An examination of the deletions and additions leaves
the general impression that he omitted some passages that attributed to Shakespeare a belief in the interpenetration of the supernatural with the natural and that he added, in particular, a
paragraph acknowledging a deficiency in Shakespeare's positive
materialism. For example, after a presentation of Shakespeare as
"a priest to us all / Of all the wonder and bloom of the world"
and as "a teacher of the hearts of men and women," he omitted
the following: ". . . one from whom may be learned something of

that inner principle that ever modulates with murmurs of the air / And motions of the forests, and the sea, / And voices of living beings, and . . . hymns, / Of night and day, and the deep heart of man."

The fundamental thought of this passage is that one learns from Shakespeare that a spiritual reality exists and vibrates harmoniously in both nature and man—that spiritual reality which Dowden named "God" in another passage also deleted from his manuscript. Though Dowden wanted to add to Shakespeare what he felt the Elizabethan lacked, he feared lest he "put too much of himself into Shakespeare"; and he deleted these passages. Yet the deficiency in Shakespeare's emphasis on the concrete needed to be pointed out; therefore, he added to the lecture notes the following: "We need to supplement the noble positivism in Shakspere with an element not easy to describe or define, but none the less actual, which the present century has demanded as essential to its spiritual life and well-being, and which its spiritual teachers— Wordsworth, Coleridge, Shelley, Newman, Maurice, Carlyle, Browning, Whitman (a strong and apparently motley assemblage!) have supplied and are still supplying. The scientific movement of the present century is not more unquestionable a fact, than this is a fact." [9] In a passage added to his discussion of Francis Bacon's philosophy in the early part of these lecture notes, he had written also that Bacon's positivism was "wanting in some spiritual elements which had not been lost sight of in earlier and darker times." [10]

What was the spiritual supplement lacking in Shakespeare, commonly taught by Wordsworth, Coleridge, Shelley, Newman, Maurice, Carlyle, Browning, and Whitman? The common bond linking Wordsworth, Coleridge, and Maurice, as presented previously, was a spiritual affinity with German Romanticism. Carlyle's right of membership in this group is also readily acknowledged. But by what common bond can Shelley, Newman, Browning, and Whitman be linked to the others as contributing towards the deficiency that Dowden found in Shakespeare's positivism? A look at the key passages exhibiting Dowden's analyses of the various contributions of these authors demonstrates that what they have in common is a prophetic summons of a materialistically minded age to spirituality. Of Shelley's place among these prophets, Dowden wrote:

Idealist as he was, Shelley lived in some important respects in closer and more fruitful relation with the real world than did his great contemporary, Scott. Because he lived with ideas, he apprehended with something like prophetic insight those great forces which have been altering the face of the world during the nineteenth century, and which we sum up under the names of democracy and science; and he apprehended them not from the merely material point of view, but from that of a spiritual being, uniting in his vision with democracy and science a third element not easy to name or to define, an element of spirituality which has been most potent, in the higher thought and feeling of our time. . . . Wordsworth, an incomparably greater thinker than Shelley, expressed a poet's fears—fears by no means wholly unjustified—that the pursuit of analytic investigation in things material might dull the eye for what is vital and spiritual in nature and in man. "Beautiful and ineffectual angel beating in the void his luminous wings in vain." No, not in the void, but amid the prime forces of the modern world; and this ineffectual angel was one of the heralds of the dawn—dawn portentous, it may be, but assuredly real.[11]

Newman is also one of the "true nineteenth-century sons of the prophets, who would make no compromises . . . in his own way [he] lifted up a solitary voice crying repentance and terror and judgment to come." His call to repentance was that

we may win a quickened sense of the reality of the invisible world, and a more strenuous resolution to live with the loins girt and the lamp lit. . . . A young Protestant heretic from America, who prized at their true worth Cardinal Newman's "Verses on Various Occasions," took courage one day and sent a copy of that volume to the Oratory at Birmingham, with a request for the writer's autograph. It was returned with the inscription, *Viriliter age, expectans Dominus*—words containing in little Newman's best contribution to his time; his vivid faith in a spiritual world, and the call to his fellows in an age of much material ease and prosperity to rise and quit them like men.[12]

Two particulars in Browning's work assign him to the place of prophet in the literary history of the nineteenth century. "First, he attempts to re-establish a harmony between what is infinite and what is finite in man's nature. . . . Secondly, what determines Mr. Browning's place in the history of our literature is that he represents militant transcendentalism, the transcendental movement at odds with the scientific." [13] Obviously, inherent in these passages is the implication that the element needed to supplement Shakespeare's positivism, in Dowden's estimation, was a divine presence in the positive facts of the world. "Shakespeare made me a citizen of the world," he confessed; "but all my vows were heard by Wordsworth." [14] And, when the greatest of the Elizabethans became too secular for the critic, he was baptized with Wordsworthianism—or Goethianism. Especially in the following passage, one of the closing paragraphs of his book, is seen the struggle in the soul of Dowden over Shakespeare's preoccupation with the earthly and its ultimate compromise:

Shakspere is the poet of concrete things and real. True, but are not those informed with passion and with thought? A time not seldom comes when a man, abandoning abstractions and metaphysical entities, turns to the actual life of the world, and to the real men and women who surround him, for the sources of emotion and thought and action —a time when *he strives to come into communion with the Unseen, not immediately, but through the revelation of the Seen*. And then he finds the strength and sustenance with which Shakspere has enriched the world.[15]

It is important to notice in these deletions and additions that Dowden's struggle to gain a clear, consistent conception of Shakespeare consists of his acknowledgment—early and late in the text —of Shakespeare as a positivist, as a poet of the concrete, as well as of his interpretation of Shakespeare's direct positivism as being indirectly a witness to transcendental truth. The contradiction— or, perhaps, the overlapping—of these aspects of his conception is immediately discernible; and its presence is a persuasive attestation to the contest of the critic with his materials.

The change in Dowden's interpretation of Shakespeare could easily be rationalized, however; for Positivism (Comte's later expression of it) and the type of Transcendental thought which Dowden entertained have in common a higher law, or moral order; and the central impulse of it is love. Positivism finds religious sanctions for its order by deifying Humanity as the Great Being worthy of worship; Transcendental idealism finds in the moral order a divine presence both in man and beyond him. That Shakespeare believed in a moral order as man's highest exercise of foresight, energy, and resolution could be interpreted by Dowden as Shakespeare's positivism. But Shakespeare was more than a humanitarian idealist; he believed also, according to Dowden, in the ontological status of that order—and that could be interpreted as his Transcendentalism.

In selecting the specific attribute of first-class works, Dowden established the standard that they be "strictly and sternly tried by their foundation in, and radiation of in the highest sense, and always indirectly, the ethic principles, and eligibility to free, arouse, dilate." [16] A surface reading of this statement pastes the label of "Positivism" above it, but a closer scrutiny indicates that the ethic principles are radiated "in the highest sense" and always "indirectly." This statement could also be interpreted to mean no more than "Literary masterpieces, even though morally informed, are not didactic." But, if the phrase "in the highest sense" refers to suprahuman efforts, ontological status is given to the "ethic principles," which in turn becomes but a metaphorical expression descriptive of the Unknown Somewhat in the world that moves indirectly through material nature toward direct moral goals.

An examination of the triple infinitives "to free, arouse, dilate," a phrase recurring in Shakspere and in other of Dowden's works, may suggest what mental associations are involved in his statement. Since the phrase was borrowed from Walt Whitman's Democratic Vistas, one may assume some similarity of Dowden's to Whitman's esthetics—enough at least to make Dowden an ardent admirer of Whitman so that he would join with Rossetti and Swinburne (poets who did not measure up to his critical standards) to oppose a public largely hostile to the American. The likeness of Whitman's to Dowden's viewpoint resided in their mutual attempt to reconcile modern science, democracy, and industrialism with a concomitant belief in the inherency of divine laws "through all and over all forever." "To spiritualize the democracy by asserting the power of a religion in harmony with modern science, has been the chief tendency of Whitman's later writings"—a statement of Dowden's that is equally true of both the American poet and the Irish critic.[17] Whitman glorified and made a religion of what was common to every man, a kind of pantheism of a democratic country, where the multitude and variety demand a counterpoise in the one and changeless.[18] "Whitman has a peculiar reason of his own for loving science," Dowden said in defense of the "poet of democracy":

he is a mystic, and such a mystic as finds positive science not un-
acceptable. Whitman beholds no visions of visible things in heaven or
hell unseen to other men. He rather sees with extraordinary precision
the realities of our earth, but he sees them, in his mystical mood, as
symbols of the impalpable and spiritual. They are hieroglyphs most
clear-cut, most brilliantly and definitely coloured to his eye, but still
expressive of something unseen. . . . From such indications as these,
and others that have gone before, the reader must gather, as best he
can, the nature of Whitman's religious faith.[19]

Here and there Dowden also associated Whitman's ideas with
Wordsworth's and with those of the famous American Transcendentalists: Emerson and Thoreau.

II *Rationalization of His Changes*

With these associations in the background, Dowden could continue the rationalization of his interpretation of Shakespeare: "If
we recognize in a moral order of the world a divine presence, then
the divine presence is never absent from the Shaksperian
world."[20] Shakespeare was one of the few men of genius, he
affirms, who was able to penetrate "*through* life at some eternal
significance of which life is the symbol." Dowden notes in *King
Richard III* that a "divine instinct," which informs men's minds of
coming danger, moves in the breasts of the citizens. Yet, throughout the greater part of Dowden's study, he presents Shakespeare
as a positivist who, aware that ultimate causes are unknown and
unknowable, endeavored to bring his intellect into fruitful relation with the positive facts of life and to abandon the dream life
of the idealist for the altruistic realism of positivism. Shakespeare's
gradual mastery of the real world Dowden traces through five
stages: (1) the early comedies and first tragedy, *Romeo and Juliet;* (2) the histories; (3) the later comedies; (4) the great tragedies and the Roman dramas; (5) and the last plays—*The Tempest, The Winter's Tale,* and *Cymbeline*.

The first period of Shakespeare's growth, Dowden points out, is
a tentative one: the period of early comedy. During these early
years of authorship, the poet had not yet achieved a firm grasp on
life, but he was aware of his deficiency and sought to eliminate it.
Love's Labour's Lost, for instance, was Shakespeare's exhortation
to "get hold of the realities of human nature and human life . . .

and found upon these realities, and not upon the mist or the air, our schemes of individual and social advancement." The youthful idealists in the court of the King of Navarre were guilty of shaping life according to notions rather than according to reality; and they therefore idealized away the facts of life. In their zeal for the idea, they had forgotten one half of themselves, the insistent demands of the senses and of the affections for fulfillment. Neither was the concern of the heroines with the practical aspects of life entirely commendable if it was isolated from the influence of ideas; for perfect culture must faithfully include both aspects of the human personality. *A Midsummer Night's Dream* also suggests the gradual establishing of an harmonious relation between imagination and actuality.

During this early period, Shakespeare also wrote his first tragedy, *Romeo and Juliet,* and pursued work on his series of historical dramas. The writing of *Romeo and Juliet* aided Shakespeare in his attempt to make a vital connection between the worlds of the ideal and the real. At first Romeo, like Shakespeare himself, is not entirely in harmony with real life: he lives in a world of imagination. He appears to be in love with Rosaline, but he is actually enamoured with the idea of love. Juliet's love, reinvigorating by its base in positive, objective fact, delivered Romeo from dream into reality: then "passion, imagination, and will fused together, and Romeo, who was weak, has at length become strong." Shakespeare's sincere and zealous efforts to bring the world of ideas into relation with the world of fact are also evident in the various styles and the diverse types with which he experimented during this period. History, comedy of incident, comedy of dialogue, comedy of sentiment, tragedy—all are attempts to put himself into relation with facts of the most diverse kinds.

During the second period, Shakespeare was "gaining a sure grasp of the positive facts of life." The world represented in the histories of this period was chiefly one of action, "the limited world of the practicable," where the measure of man is his deeds. The study of history, the deliberate confrontation of the poet's mind with everyday facts, further enabled the poet to overcome his own excessive passion and thought, his chief weaknesses, and to build up his own moral nature, thereby fortifying himself for the conduct of life.

The kings who failed in the positive, material world of these histories were those who looked away from life as it is toward their own notions or ideals—King John, Richard II, Henry VI, and Richard III. King John "endeavored to turn away his eyes from facts of which he is yet aware": his house was built on the sands of selfishness, rottenness, and shame—a detrimental fact which, uncorrected, should rightly remove the crown from his head. Richard II also failed to lay hold of things as they are: "He has a kind of artistic relation to life, without being an artist. An artist in life seizes upon the stuff of circumstances, and, with strenuous will and strong creative power, shapes some new and noble form of human existence." What an artist must possess—co-ordination, power of will, and imagination—Richard lacked.

Henry VI, the timid king, nurtured in himself a saintliness not related to reality. His crime was egoism, "the egoism of timid saintliness," characterized by a passivity which avoids engagement in active virtue. The indictment of Henry VI by the great Duke of York confirms one's sense of fact and right, continues Dowden: " 'King did I call thee? Nay, thou art not king. / Give place; by heaven thou shalt rule no more / O'er him whom heaven created for thy ruler!' " Richard III, the terrifying but fascinating embodiment of the demonic, inverted the moral order of the world against whose outraged laws he dashed himself to pieces. However, Richmond, who is expressly the champion and representative of the moral order of the world—an aspect Richard had endeavored to set aside—overcame him.

Henry IV, on the other hand, succeeded because his was a strong, finite character who attained a measure of practical mastery of the world. In him, there was nothing infinite, to be sure: no exultant faith in God, no strong reliance upon principles. He, too, was therefore, incomplete; and his success was but partial since he "penetrated only a little way among the facts of life." His son, Henry V, however, most gloriously succeeded in a practical mastery of the world. In fact, all the characters of the histories lead up to Henry V. The central element in his character was "a noble realization of fact." Through the union of his personal resources with the vital strength of the world, he became one of its most glorious and beneficent forces. The chief characteristic of the close of this second period was Shakespeare's own progress in self-possession and mastery of his powers. Like his creatures, the creator had established a vital connection with the positive, practical world; but also like Henry V, successful as Shakespeare was in accepting and adjusting to the material side of life, he had not yet come to terms with the evil and ugly aspects of existence.

Between the periods of the histories and the tragedies, Shakespeare wrote his brightest and loveliest comedies—*The Taming of the Shrew, The Merry Wives of Windsor, Much Ado About Nothing, As You Like It*, and *Twelfth Night*. The essential characteristic of this time is the freedom of Shakespeare's laughter and the contrast it provides to the dark period of the tragedies which follow. He had put aside concentration on the historical, but he had not yet fallen under the influence of the tragic in life. The transition between the periods of the histories and tragedies marks the increase in Shakespeare's revolt against the world which found less to arouse his indignation when he was thirty or thirty-five years of age than when he was forty. That is, Shakespeare's attempt to adjust the two halves of himself was not without its season of frustration and rebellion, when the spiritual half was out of harmony with the material half. Only during the period of the last plays was he to attain serenity and to regain his mirth by proper adjustment of these two halves of himself.

The fourth period contains the great tragedies, the theme of which, unlike that of the histories, was not material success or failure, but spiritual fulfillment or failure according to "a destiny higher than that which is related to the art of getting on in life." Shakespeare wished to exemplify the necessity of a due balance in men's nature, a just equipoise between the sensational and intellectual faculties, between the impulses of their passions and the laws of their intelligence. In the tragic failure of these dramas, this balance was disturbed. In Hamlet, for instance, the images of his fancy were far more vivid than his actual perception. Macbeth, Iago, and Edmund were also among those who rationalized away the consciousness of most sacred obligations. Their intellects —hard, skeptical, and unmoved by the instinctual restraints of the heart—led them not to virtue but to crime.

In contrast to Macbeth, Iago, and Edmund is Kent, a man with a balanced nature, whose emotions are held in just balance by reason, yet whose will is motivated by a deep instinct of the heart to loyalty. In those who do good, like Kent, the head is guided by the heart; and the heart, by the head. Thought, obscurely present in instinctive action and in human emotion, vitalizes and inspires these men rather than tyrannically dominates them, as Dowden states later. Overdependence of the individual on the energies either of the intellect or of the passions is a disease of the soul—a malady which Shakespeare sought consciously to avoid himself and the symptoms of which he diagnosed carefully for his readers. Romeo and Hamlet are examples of the extremes, for each failed to maintain the will in a fruitful relation with facts: Romeo, because he brooded over things as they mirrored themselves in his own emotions; Hamlet, because he viewed them as they reflected themselves in his own thinking. Because Hamlet's ideas were more real than his perceptions, he was able only to resolve, not to act. No matter how excellent were Hamlet's faculties of intellect, they cannot be considered valuable if they do not lead Hamlet to involvement in the real world; for the great object of life cannot be realized by reflective or speculative activities alone; the kind of truth to which the complete man is committed is realized truth.

Brutus also failed because moral ideas and principles were more valuable to him than concrete realities. As an idealist, he lived among books, nourished himself with philosophy, and secluded himself from involvement with concrete realities. Brutus's view of life was lopsided because it was "not imaginative or pictorial or dramatic, but wholly ethical." Antony's view suffered by being wholly aesthetic and sensual; he had abandoned a complete view of reality by yielding to an inordinate passion for pleasure. As a result, he failed to allow for a "certain inevitable fact—a law above beauty and pleasure by which they should be regulated and integrated into life." Both Brutus and Antony, therefore, were destined to fail in the positive world. If duty be the motivating ideal of Brutus, and pleasure the ideal of Antony, that which motivated Coriolanus was an ideal of self-centered power. Just as Antony betrayed himself by laxity and indulgence, Coriolanus violated his soul by rigidity and pride. All of these characters give abundant evidence, Dowden concludes, that Shakespeare comprehended the weakness of his own tendency to idealize away the facts and that he worked with an energetic will towards the transfusion of his knowledge into facts.

In Dowden's presentation of this period of Shakespeare's development, he discusses at some length the problem of evil, a discussion which, because of traces of his inner conflict with his subject

—traces where he "put some of himself into Shakespeare in self-defense"—should be indicated. He rejects the possibility of interpreting evil as an outward expression of inward temptation. The weird sisters in *Macbeth* are not simply the objective correlative of inward temptation; much more than this, they are embodiments of the demonic forces of the world which exist independently of man. Just as there is a salvatory "stream of virtuous force, a beneficent current," which bears us onward toward joy, purity, and sacrifice, so there is a countercurrent which "drifts us towards darkness and cold and death." In this prose Dowden presents evil and good as essential comates as he does in his poem, "La Révélation Par Le Désert." In interpreting *Timon of Athens,* the last of the tragedies, Dowden also asserts that knowledge of evil is necessary to discovery of good.

Early in Dowden's discussion these benevolent and malevolent forces are presented as the accumulated creation of the human race; for, although the forces of evil and good are outside men, they are produced, to be sure, in the social medium in which men live and move. The existence of such forces is at once "scientifically accurate" but beyond "demonstrable knowledge." Despite Dowden's sincerity of effort to present good and evil within the limits of the positive world of Shakespeare, the discussion spills over into the realm of faith and religion: the titles "devil" and "God" are given to the evil and the good powers in the world to whom men render service.[21] These titles for good and evil could be explained as metaphorical if it were not for Dowden's conjecture elsewhere of the existence in the moral order of the world of a Divine Presence, a proposition which necessarily shifts the interpretation of Shakespeare's world away from a position of strict Positivism. What Dowden says of good and evil in *Shakspere* is also similar to what he has said elsewhere in his works: good and evil are a mingled web, and Shakespeare separates the threads to observe each one. Evil is abnormal, but the sources of good are incalculable and ultimately triumphant.

A fifth period of Shakespeare's development is, to Dowden, noticeable in the last plays—*The Tempest, The Winter's Tale,* and *Cymbeline.* During this period Shakespeare's temper demanded a denouement of joy or peace. Shakespeare determined that he would resolve the dissonance of the tragedies, which expresses, first of all, his own spiritual struggles, and that he would mold his own temperament to harmonize with the existing facts and laws of the world and thereby bring to himself a measure of quietness. Like his characters Hermione, Imogen, and Prospero, their creator finally learned to accept the inevitability of evil, to struggle actively against it, and to overcome it because he had learned to forgive. Like the wronged sufferers of the last plays, Shakespeare may still feel the pain of the tragic in life; but he has triumphed over resentment, hatred, and bitterness by his submission to a higher law of life.

Prospero, the character with whose mood Shakespeare's own may be most clearly identified, is the man of genius; he is also the great artist who at first lacks the practical grasp of material facts which would assure his success. But, due to his experience on the island, he finally subjected to his will both "the spirits of the elements [symbolic of the ideal half of himself], and Caliban, the gross genius of brute matter [symbolic of the material half of himself]"; and thus he gained complete possession of himself—a development necessary to his subsequent performance as a successful ruler. Harmony between head and heart is necessary not only for the realization of the mature adulthood of Prospero but also for the making of great artists like Shakespeare.

Here and there throughout *Shakspere*, Dowden characterizes Shakespeare's growth, development, and maturity as identical with his submission to "a higher law." What Dowden means by the phrase "a higher law" and its equivalents should be defined to obtain the full significance of the last paragraph of *Shakspere*, in which Dowden concludes that Shakespeare, primarily a positivist ("We are still out of doors"), has not supplied the reader with either a doctrine, an interpretation, or a revelation. What he has contributed is "courage and energy and strength to dedicate himself and his work to whatever it be which life has revealed to him as *best and highest and most real*." There are at least two places in Dowden's publications that explicitly define these expressions: one appears in his introductory remarks on Oliver Goldsmith in Thomas Humphry Ward's *English Poets* (1890); the other, in a letter written in 1906.[22] In the essay on Goldsmith, the "higher self" is equated with the affections and with the imagination, which, in the 1906 letter, becomes equivalent to "God's immediate presence in the soul."

In summation, Dowden presents Shakespeare not only as a poet of the concrete and real world, but also as a revealer of "a Somewhat" of which the concrete and real are manifestations. The discovery that Shakespeare's viewpoint was as deeply moral as it was esthetic afforded Dowden grounds for interpreting him as a witness, though an indirect one, to the ultimate Good inherent in the universe, of the Divine interpenetrating the finite.

CHAPTER 5

His Aloofness from the Irish Literary Renaissance

> And I wanted to point out that much
> of the best work is not ascribed to the
> glebe, but if rooted in any soil, lives
> in a wider spiritual world.—Dowden,
> *Letters*, p. 241.

I *The Problem*

ONE of the chief problems challenging the student of Edward Dowden is his failure to support, or even to interpret, the literary Renaissance of his country that occurred during the last decade of the century when he was at the peak of his own literary power. His failure to recognize his countrymen's literary efforts could perhaps be explained had he been a critic of less stature: but Dowden was a conscientious scholar whose life was thoroughly and devotedly integrated with his studies, and he was the most outstanding literary critic in Ireland, one who was not only recognized and honored locally for his superior achievements but also acknowledged and esteemed internationally. Yet his response to the Celtic revival was negative; his attitude was an enigma to his Irish literary friends, an incomprehensibility that at first mystified and then estranged them.

When the National Society of Dublin was formed, Dowden's name was absent from its roster of members, though there were signatures of his contemporaries, some of whom were his friends and some his students. When the Irish Literary Theater was established, his name was missing from the lists of both guarantors and contributors, but some colleagues from Trinity College were guarantors. When Thomas Moore's centenary was celebrated, Dowden remained aloof. When invited to submit some of his poetry for *A Treasury of Irish Poetry*, he was reluctant: "What I have written has really no right to appear in a specially Irish An-

127

thology, and if anything worth living is in it, it comes out of the
mother, Earth; so I should be content to be one of a general
crowd of small singers rather than one of a local group." [1] Such
seeming indifference to Irish literature seemed all the more
strange to its advocates because of Dowden's enthusiastic admiration and defense of an American poet, who was outstanding for
his emphasis on a nationalistic literature—Walt Whitman. Such
seeming inconsistencies in Dowden were reprehensible to his Irish
friends; there was something disconcerting to the Irish mind in
Dowden's eager acceptance of a Whitman to the literary canon
but his blind rejection of a Yeats.

Several explanations of the possible causes of Dowden's bypass-
ing of Irish literature have been given. H. O. White, recently re-
tired from the chair of English literature in Dublin University,
which Dowden had formerly held, suggests that Dowden's curious blindness to the significance of the contemporary revival of
Irish literature could be explained both by his strong political
opinions and by his view of literature as essentially cosmopolitan. [2] Occupied with the perspective of the literature of the world,
Dowden failed to see the full import of the literature of his own
back yard. Ernest Augustus Boyd, a younger contemporary, finds
the cause in the fact that Dowden was a "half-breed Irishman":
his parents were Protestant, he was educated in schools of the
English tradition, he was salaried as professor by one of these
schools, and this Anglicized background predisposed him to prefer England to his native land. To Boyd, "the artificial barriers set
up by the Anglicized culture" closed the door forever to Dowden
and those of like mind to an understanding and appreciation of
Irish culture. Boyd also proposes, though less convincingly, that
Dowden's neglecting to support the Irish Renaissance poetry with
critical studies was contributory to its failure to appeal widely.
But a counterproposal to Boyd's could be made: a movement mer-
iting wide appeal is surely not so severely hampered by the lack of
support of the single voice of even a distinguished critic.

More mildly critical of Dowden than Boyd, John Eglinton (the
pseudonym adopted by William Kilpatrick Magee, an Irish essay-
ist)—the only contributor to Celtic literature whom Dowden
really lamented not having written about—does not think that the
cause of Dowden's disassociation from the Irish literary revival
resides solely in the unfortunate political situation of Ireland,

though the Union of Ireland with the British Commonwealth, he admits, was a contributing factor. Eglinton, suggesting a more complex explanation, adds two other constituents to the possible cause—one geographical and the other esthetic. Dowden lived in the Eastern province of Ireland, a locality favorable equally for visits to the manufacturing cities of England and for wanderings through the "fair field of Holy Ireland," a geographical situation contributory to congenial relations and closer ties with the English. The opportunities intrinsic in such a region for cultural cross-fertilization naturally tended to Anglicize its residents to a greater degree than the less frequent contacts of the English with the Western Irish. To this geographical consideration, and possibly as an outgrowth of it, may be connected another reason; an esthetic one. The crux of the difference between Dowden and the Nationalists, Eglinton claims, was his insistent view "that literature, like religion, is essentially international." [4] Eglinton's suggestion that Dowden's literary isolation was rooted, not in his politics, but in a necessary and consistent application of his view of life and literature seems a better explanation of Dowden's denial of support to the Irish Renaissance artists.

There are plausible elements in each explanation. It is true that the role Dowden played as a politician—as already delineated in Chapter One—was so vigorous and intense that it is little wonder the Nationalist artists believed his literary theory was predetermined by his politics. What the Nationalist artists failed to see was the integral relationship between Dowden's response to the Celtic Revival and his world-view. Yet neither political affinity, as Ernest Boyd holds, nor geographical location, as John Eglinton affirms, is the primary consideration that prompted Dowden's withdrawal. Instead, the reason lies in a basic philosophical difference which includes, of course, the esthetic difference which Eglinton also points out. Dowden's aloofness from the Irish Literary Renaissance was consistent with his view of life and literature; his reticence to encourage or contribute to the movement was the practical expression of his literary theory. The three basic tendencies of the Movement—the Celtic, the nationalistic, and the esoteric—were incompatible with his own viewpoint: Celticism, because of its function as the green banner of nationalism; nationalism, because of its narrow exclusiveness; and subjectivism, because of its blindness to the truths of science.

II   Difference between Dowden and the Two Leaders
of the Irish Renaissance: Yeats and George Russell (AE)

The Irish imaginative movement was attached chiefly to the name of W. B. Yeats, who managed persistently to maintain its leadership and whose views, both influenced by and influencing those of George Russell (AE)—poet, mystic, and classmate of Yeats at art school—contributed to its characteristic coloring. Both young men were just starting their careers in the 1890s, and both were seeking for a unified concept of life that would give meaning to the chaotic facts of experience. Though both these leaders were to modify their early views, it is their life and thought before Dowden's death in 1913 that would have motivated his response to the movement that they influenced and encouraged. This chapter, therefore, is confined chiefly to that period.

The difference between Dowden's viewpoint and that of the two leaders of the Renaissance rests more in the subject matter of art and in the creative process than in nationalism or in cosmopolitanism. While both Dowden and his opponents emphasize traditional matter as essential to great poetry, their concepts of tradition vary radically. Tradition, to Yeats and Russell, is more mythical and legendary, more oral than written, and more concerned with the past than with the heritage of the present.

Yeats reacted alike to the rationalism bequeathed by the eighteenth century and to the scientific movement of the nineteenth. He hated science and industrialism, longed for a return of Ireland to the heroic values of the past, and hence fostered the Celtic revival. He envisioned the creation of a heroic, passionate concept of life based on the folklore of the uneducated in Ireland, which through poetry and art might be made a subject worthy of study among the educated in all countries and which might also become a political passion unifying the Irish people. The catalyst he used in hope of bringing about such a change was the irrational: magic, Theosophy, Cabala, Spiritualism, folklore, and evoked moods.

In the 1890s Yeats hoped to found a magical society in Ireland, the Irish Mystical Order, which would integrate Gaelic with Greek myth, Theosophical dogma, nationalism, and various esoteric creeds. In 1896 he went to Paris to prepare the ritual for the order that he hoped would cause the Irish to come to venerate their native land instead of Judea as holy. Yeats's belief rested in his hope of founding a school of poets, an idea abhorrent to most poets. In this regard, Eglinton has said of Yeats: "The notion of a 'school' of poets is congenial to him; and indeed, if he could have his way, I think he would make of the whole profession of litera-ture one vast secret order, training its novices in the occult sci-ences and instructing them in a system of symbolic images, some-what as they seem to have done in the bardic colleges of ancient Ireland." [5]

A Romantic when Romanticism was in its final extravagance, Yeats's goal was at first "the deliberate creation of a kind of Holy City of the imagination," which, as he wrote in *Dramatis Per-sonae,* would provide a rapturous existence, immutable and eter-nal, to which the soul might be transported. Yeats gave it the names of "the happy townland," "the glittering town," and "the predestined dancing-place." Perhaps Dowden was surreptitiously discrediting Yeats's cloud-Paradise when he wrote in his biogra-phy of Robert Browning: "But there are times when perhaps the choice lies only between conservation of what is imperfect and the attempt to erect an airy fabric which has no basis upon the solid earth; and Browning on the whole preferred a veritable *civitas hominum,* however remote from the ideal, to a sham *civitas Dei* or a real Cloud-cuckootown." [6]

The regenerate patriotism that Yeats desired was based on a relation of man to the state. Aware of the general intellectual defi-ciency and the beaten patriotism of the Irish people, he had hoped, as he recorded in *Letters to the New Island* (1934), that a remedy might be to "unite literature to the great passion of patri-otism and ennoble both thereby." Men found the mark of great-ness in poets, he came to believe, when "everything they see has its relation to the national life, and through that to the universal and divine life." The unity of all is, thus, to be found in the state, the free recognition of which by poets, as by prophets of the people, would bring ultimate harmony.

This concept is also the thesis of George Russell's essay, *The National Being* (1918), a handbook of mystic nationalism: the state is "the physical body prepared for the incarnation of the soul of the race." The state is the "greater life," "the National Being," the "oversoul" to which the individual freely submits; it, in turn,

influences the life of the individual; a life within his life, it molds
his spirit to its likeness. Both Yeats and Russell believed in an
aristocracy of culture would lead Ireland towards such an ideal.
Russell felt that the national spirit itself was a spiritual force
which, having begun among his Irish predecessors, revealed itself
in poetry and legend, and was working even in his own times to
incarnate itself fully, perhaps within a generation, if there could
be unity among the intellectuals on fundamentals.[7] "Every Irishman forms some vague ideal of his country, born from his reading
of history, or from contemporary politics, or from an imaginative
intuition," he wrote in "Nationality and Cosmopolitanism in Literature" (1899); "and this Ireland in the mind it is, not the actual
Ireland, which kindles his enthusiasm." The objective Ireland of
wood, mountain, and lake is to Russell but the shadowy expression of the mind of God. Because of his esoteric belief, Ireland
was also "Holy" to Russell; for Ireland was one of the few locali-
ties of the world where the Earth has been especially recognized
by its ancient bards as a divine beng, as the Mighty Mother.[8]

The persuasiveness of this conviction led Russell to mount the
seawall one Sunday afternoon on the esplanade at Bray and to tell
the curious crowd that "the golden age was all about them, that
the earth underfoot was sacred as Judea. . . ."[9] By a determined
effort he hoped to mold the ideals of the people by fostering his
country's latent spirituality. Like Yeats, he envisioned a nation of
Irishmen not enslaved to materialism but motivated by the revived splendors and ideals of the imaginative world of Irish legend. Irish ideals were to be, he wrote in a letter to Yeats, the
return to the heroic and legendary Ireland and the recall from
that early time of the "great, vast, and ennobling."

Russell recalled in *The Candle of Vision* (1919) how he had sat
for hours in concentration on the old Druid remains while waiting
for visions of the other world. By an intense exercise of will and
by a passionate longing for the ancestral self, he believed, there
would come forth from the depths of the Earth glimpses of a life
more rapturous than those of everyday experience. By such asceticism man could apprehend the supernal. Though some visions
might not come without ascetic efforts, they could nonetheless be
evoked by a conscious effort of the will. Men are gods in exile, he
claimed, who have descended to earth from primordial substance
and who, thereby, have lost their ethereal character and settled

into a solid or static condition. For every man on earth there is a divinity in the heavens who is his "Ancestral Self"; but "the will has not yet found its conscious root in the power which sustains the cosmos." [10]

The recovery of this lost glory, both for himself and for others, was Russell's mission; and his poems are efforts to point the way "Homeward." It was Russell who assured Yeats of the sacredness of their common mission to revive interest in Celtic legend. In a letter of February 6, 1896, he stated to Yeats his belief that the gods had returned to Ireland as seen by some in visions and as evidenced by purple color flashing and reflecting here and there over the Irish hills. Their return, he continued, had already revived the ancient faith in fairies and Druids. He also prophesied that a new incarnation of deity was about to appear in Ireland, one whom he himself had seen in a vision and would recognize upon his appearance. As a result of his belief, Russell urged Yeats to return to County Sligo to witness these manifestations of magical and divine power.[11] In Dublin, Russell claimed to have seen the ancient gods of Ireland on a certain hilltop which could be viewed from Dowden's windows. In writing about the event a decade later, Dowden facetiously remarked: "As for fairies they have all been exported to the London market . . . I am afraid they [the ancient gods], too, are getting tinned . . . for exportation." [12]

The necessity of stringent measures to obtain contact with the supernal, such as Russell practiced, Dowden would deny. Russell's asceticism, which starves the senses, was to Dowden a denial of half of the human capability. Such asceticism severs the relation between the visible and the invisible; it creates a gulf between sense and spirit; and man ceases to be able to realize his full humanity. To Russell, and to Yeats as well, the visible was somewhat antagonistic to the invisible; but to Dowden the visible and the invisible were only different aspects of one great reality.

Though an out-of-the-world vision like Russell's found little room for acceptance in Dowden's mind, Yeats was sympathetic with it; and he confessed in his *Autobiographies* (1926) that, when a lad of eighteen, he had seen mysterious fires at Rosses and Knocknarea, as he had previously by the river at Ballisodare. Another promoter of the Celtic movement, George Moore, a frequent companion of Russell on some of his vision-seeking bicycle rides around the countryside, was, like Dowden, less credulous. On some trips Moore waited several hours while Russell, in deep concentration, sat cross-legged seeking a vision of the gods in a Druidic circle or atop a hill. And, when Russell reported the subsequent failure, due to interference with the spirits of the atmosphere by unbelieving presences—two Presbyterian ministers on one occasion, for example—Moore was not surprised.[13] Another friend who doubted, John Eglinton, reported in his essay on "AE and His Story": ". . . one listened a little uneasily sometimes to the narration of his encounters with lofty beings who occasionally 'spake unto him.' " [14]

Dowden opposed the mythical and legendary view of tradition which motivated Yeats and Russell. To Dowden, tradition has more to do with scientifically accurate history than with myth, more with the written than with the oral. And, though the poet should be faithful to the best traditions, Dowden believed, he should not be in subjection to them; instead, he should profit from them and press forward to those noble goals towards which tradition and men together work. If the Irish poet-antiquary would study, said Dowden, traditional material with the resources of modern science, he would "lead us towards truth instead of plunging us in folly and illusion." [15] For the poet to attempt to revive old faiths is as "feebly wild as that of drawing a curtain of worn-out shreds to hide the risen sun of science." [16] To the advocates of the Renaissance, literature should mirror the glorious age of the past; but, to Dowden, it should reflect the contemporary life, which is comprised by the contributions of the past as well as by the promise of the future. Though both sides call for faithfulness to the past, each strangely ignores the truths of the past inherent in the other's position; for Yeats and AE ignore the ties of the Irish with the English, and Dowden bypasses completely the uniquely Irish past. Essentially, however, their differences of viewpoint in regard to tradition are due to the disparity between their respective cyclical and linear views of history; for Yeats and Russell believed in truth as eternally recurring, whereas Dowden believed in it as progressively unfolding.

Their differences extend as well to the manner in which literature is produced. Both Yeats and AE judge things first and last as they appeal to the imagination and emotion. Endeavoring to locate values as far away as possible from those of science and materialism, they focus at this time exclusively on otherworldly ideal-ism. For them, beauty, the sole aim of art, is a disembodied ideal, intuitively apprehended. Both Yeats and Russell equated imagina-tion with "the essence of personality, and already the denizen of a world in which it can converse with like spiritual essences and even hold communion with the dead." [17] Both believed also in the magical power of symbolism to recall "moods long ago felt of spir-itual sincerity and aspiration," which would bring the poet in con-tact with the supernal. Yeats's *The Celtic Twilight* (1893) tells of communications from "those beings or bodiless moods, or what-ever they are that inhabit the world of spirits." [18] Yeats was never sure, however, whether the imagination created these moods or only evoked them. Once created—whether by the artist, by the great memory of which men's minds and memories are a part, or merely by the association of material and spiritual things—"sym-bols . . . are taken into the great mind forever, and are forever capable, if thrown out by this great mind, of planting thoughts, moods, and motives in the souls of men who contemplate them. These symbols, in the view of the symbolists, transcend particular time and place, pass beyond death, and in a sense become immor-tal souls." [19] Yeats wrote in an early essay, "The Autumn of the Body," that art was about to assume what had formerly been the prerogatives and responsibilities of religion. Art as a form of magic as a sort of alchemy would realize the moods which would effect the regeneration of the Irish; therefore, he sought his rhythms and imagery more and more in visions or in the obscure world of necromancy and séances. "No wonder," continued his contemporary John Eglinton, "that Yeats and his friend A. E. who could conjure up the mighty heroes of Celtic lore and make of Erin's mysterious past part of that Eternal Moment of which the artist is the artificer—no wonder that they believed in Irish litera-ture! And indeed it was this mystical Ireland, beheld clairvoy-antly, an Ireland sunk in ancient memories, which turned out to be the real one!" [20]

Initiated into an order of the Golden Dawn of Christian Caba-lists, Yeats had learned from a fellow student "how to allow his reveries to drift, following the suggestions of the symbol, and he was soon able to summon images from, as he thought, a deeper source than conscious or unconscious memory. He found that these images began to affect his writing making it more sensuous and vivid; and he believed that with the images would come more profound states of the soul." [21] In his trust in the ability of human faculties to penetrate into the hidden recesses of the supersensory realms of Nature and in his confidence that by magic the human spirit could exercise lordship over Nature, the mystic and the mage, though unlike, became one in Yeats. The mystic by austere discipline and by intense concentration enabled him to acquire not only self-mastery but mastery also over Nature, wherever Nature limits or obstructs the aspiring spirit of man.

Similarly influenced, chiefly by Eastern religions but especially by Theosophy, Russell believed that the truths recorded by Eastern sages appeared also to ancient Irish seers and bards and that such an authoritative wisdom was still available to those who would seek it. In *The Candle of Vision* he postulates, for instance, the probability of the imagination as psychic bodies inhering in the physical, "ethereal," "unsleeping" creatures, whose constant power and presence men lost when they were separated from the Self-Ancestral, "the being of the Ever Living." The homesickness of the spirit for identity again with the Ever Living is the theme of Russell's *Homeward Songs* (1894). This belief has poetic precedence in the Platonic concept of the preexistence of the soul and in the mythical speculations of Medieval theologians who affirmed that the soul restlessly seeks to regain the ecstasy experienced when first in contact with its Creator.

The common belief of Yeats and Russell is expressed in a letter of August 13, 1894,[22] of Russell to Dowden; in it, Russell protested the professor's criticism of *Homeward Songs*. Similarly, in a protest to Dowden a week earlier Russell had written that only the pure ascetic could develop any worthwhile spiritual acumen.[23] Dowden had censured Russell's use of the word "Brahma," had applied the adjective "cheap" to Eastern mysticism, and had rebuked Russell's failure to unite the spiritual with the material. Russell's protest is a clear statement of the polarity of their respective positions, and, more importantly, it contains not only the germ of the opposition between Dowden and the Renaissance sympathizers in general and Yeats and Russell in particular but also the philosophic and religious foundations of the Irish Renaissance as Dowden must have understood them. First, there is the antirational trust of the movement in the poet's intuitive grasp of reality, the withdrawal from nature to a self-existent activity, and the bold faith in basing art on the imagination rather than on a rational observation of the external world. Second, there is the confidence of Eastern mysticism that man comes nearer to God by self-inflicted asceticism. Third, there is the belief in the magical power of symbol: certain words like *Om, Brahma,* or *Christ* have power akin to magic incantation to recall ancient moods of spiritual earnestness and hope.

In a somewhat sportive letter in 1902, Russell told Yeats of a hysterical lady who accused him of practicing the Black Art on the audience when he chanted his drama, *Deirdre.*[24] She claimed to see "three black waves of darkness rolling down over the stage and audience." Facetiously, Russell continued that he would work in "more magic" the next time. When Russell and Yeats, sitting in Yeats's kitchen, used to chant their verses to each other after the rest of the family had gone to bed, "it was supposed upstairs that they were trying to disincarnate themselves."[25] So considered, the symbol to both Yeats and Russell was a useful weapon in their opposition to modernism. The poet, they believed, became a great magician who by his symbols conjured up immortal moods to work their will with man.

Another aspect of the otherworldly interests of Yeats and Russell was their common fascination with the landscapes of art rather than of reality, a fascination which hampered their observation of the features of nature as they are. They did not seem to see nature really, and the awareness of such blindness prompted Russell to comment: "Yet we must not become one-sided and blind to the outside world. I think spirituality without wisdom is almost as bad as utter materialism."[26] Such awareness also prompted Yeats to the soul-searching confession in a letter to Katharine Tynan in 1888: "I have noticed something about my poetry I did not know before . . . for instance, that it is almost all a flight into fairyland from the real world, and a summons to that flight."[27] In an essay entitled "The Poet of Shadows," Russell described the siren call of Yeats's fairyland on himself and others: "I have looked with longing eyes into this world. It is Ildathack, the Many-Coloured Land . . . the most beautiful of all the isles the mystic voyagers have found during the thousand years of literature recorded in Ireland. What wonder that many wish to follow him, and already other voices are singing amid its twilights."[28]

A few months later Yeats also confessed his need to substitute the landscapes of nature and human feelings and longings for those of art.[29] Later he wrote: "I have always felt that the soul has two movements primarily: one to transcend forms, and the other to create forms. Nietzsche, to whom you [John Quinn] have been the first to introduce me, calls these the Dionysiac and the Apollonian respectively. I think I have to some extent got weary of the wild god Dionysus, and I am hoping that the Far-Darter will come in his place." [30] That is, Yeats was now endeavoring to conjoin imagination and intellect as cooperatively relaying truth because he recognized that his obsession with the dreamworld of his imagination was removing him more and more from ordinary human experience.

For Dowden, on the other hand, beauty, truth, and goodness inseparably inherent in the nature of all life, both subjective and objective, are apprehended by the reciprocal cooperation of intellect, imagination, and emotion—by the whole man. Hence, the esthetic experience to Dowden is also a necessarily spiritual or moral experience consisting of the unity of spiritual and material forces, yet always reaching beyond both to the "light that never was on sea or land."

Dowden would have approved the change taking place in Yeats during the first decade of the twentieth century, a change which Yeats's father, however, forcefully opposed. The poet son seemingly had expressed to his father a doubt concerning the complete subjectivity of the creative experience and had admitted an attraction to a view of organic harmony of the subjective and objective, such as Goethe and Dowden held. Yeats's father protested in a letter to his son: "The English admiration for strong will, etc., is really part of the gospel of materialism and money-making and Empire-building. . . . You would be a *philosophe* and you are really a poet. The men whom Nietzsche's theory fits are only great men of a sort, a sort of Yahoo greatness. The struggle is how to get rid of them. . . . You are haunted by the Goethe idea, interpreted by Dowden, that a man must be a complete man. It is a chimera, a man can only be a specialist." [31] This letter reveals not only the father's criticism of the son but also an enduring difference between the father and his old friend, Dowden—a conflict of opinion which, on a personal level, corresponds to the antagonism on a public level between Dowden and those who would cultivate the Irish movement.

Early in 1872 Dowden first sensed the difference between his own view and that of J. B. Yeats. He had refrained from sending some new poems to him, "partly because he would not care for my more recent way of feeling. Positivist art would please him, or strangely different art like Blake's." [32] Two years later, Dowden wrote: "Another surprise was to find myself on absolutely equal terms with Mr. Yeats. He used to have a power of attracting undercurrents of my being in strange ways. But now I feel that I stand upon my own pinpoint of the Universe. For him the ethical disappears in the aesthetic." [33] Dowden diagnosed here the basic difference between his view of art and the elder Yeats's—and later W.B.'s—as having to do with the relationship between the "positivist art" and the "strangely different art like Blake's" or between "the ethical" and "the aesthetic." One might substitute, for the sake of explanation, the terms "natural" and "ideal," or "conscience" or "will" and "imagination." According to Dowden, J. B. Yeats wavered between the extremes of Naturalism and Romanticism.

The accuracy of Dowden's observation is justified by comparing it with the elder Yeats's criticism of his son's friendship with Russell: "He [Russell] has no love, no admiration for the individual man. He is too religious to care for really mortal things, or rather, for he does care, to admire and love them. . . . You can only pretend it—your interest is in mundane things, and Heaven to you is this world made better, whether beyond the stars or not." [34] The son's concentration on the occult, rather than on the natural world, first caused a breach between father and son. One cannot help wondering whether the father, who liked "strangely different art like Blake's," recognized the inconsistency of his position in rejecting his son's Blake-like visions. Such an inconsistency would account for the seeming contradiction of the two expressions of J.B.'s opinion and the wavering of his position as noticed by Dowden.

The second difference between Dowden and J.B. that Dowden noted was that "for him [J.B.] the ethical disappears in the aesthetic." With Dowden, the ethical has to do with the conscience or will, that faculty of the human mind that determines action in the practical world; the esthetic is used in reference to the imagination, the faculty which explores by a cooperation of intellect and intuition the depths of human experience: the living bond between the concrete and the ideal worlds. Hence, what Dowden objected to was J.B.'s failure to tie Goodness to earthly relationships—the same objection Dowden had to Matthew Arnold's "stream of tendency not ourselves effecting righteousness." In this particular, the son was evidently influenced by the father; for he too was indifferent to, or even disliked, that aspect of personality one calls "will" or "character." J. B. Yeats believed admiration for a strong will to be a malady of the English and their disciples, the Anglo-Irish; for it was a part of the despised "gospel . . . of Empire-building." The poet, J. B. believed, is outside morals and laws: "All ethical systems yet invented are a similar denial of liberty: that is why the true poet is neither moral nor religious." [35] Similarly, W.B. wrote that the morality of art is "personal, knows little of any general law." [36]

II *"The Dowden Controversy"*

The difference of opinions between Dowden and the leaders of the Irish Renaissance first became public on January, 1895, when a lecture on Sir Samuel Ferguson, "the authentic precursor of the Revival," previously delivered to the Irish Literary Society of London by Roden Noel was read in Dublin. Dowden, among others, was to make a speech about it; and his remarks provoked unintentionally a literary controversy. The *Daily Express* reported that Dowden "did not believe in an Irish literary renaissance. Of course he does not," the article continued; "how could anyone do so who thinks that an Irish poet is born out of due time because he is not acceptable to contemporary English taste, or to that small Irish circle of polite and cultivated people who know more and think more of every third, fourth, fifth, and sixth rate poet than they would of Homer himself if he lived on the Hill of Howth and wrote the epics of the Gael?" [37] "Professor Dowden expressed scorn for the Irish Literature movement and Irish literature generally," Yeats reported later to a friend, "from which he has been catching it from all the Dublin papers." [38]

Twenty-one years before, Dowden had similarly scorned Irish endeavor when, at a meeting of the Fortnightly Club, he was asked to propose the health of the Lord Lieutenant of Ireland and the welfare of Ireland. "I did my best," he recorded later, "and tried to make a little joke about the Liffey [river in Dublin] which had taken me some days to invent, and on the subject of Ireland I asked some unpractical questions such as 'Had a census been taken of the wise men in Ireland?' 'How much thought was annually spun?' 'Which passions were imported from the Continent?' and 'What were the exports of sweetness and light?' " [39] These same objections were to arouse the ire of those who encouraged Irish literature; for in these remarks one recognizes Dowden's concern lest Irish literature isolate itself from the beneficent influences of other literatures, his emphasis on the place of the intellect in the creation of imaginative literature, and his insistence on the inclusion in literature of the moral law.

The Saturday issues of the *Daily Express* in Dublin carried the controversy to the public in its columns—short articles reprinted by the *Express* office several years later as *The Literary Ideals of Ireland* (1899). W. B. Yeats and AE, John Eglinton and William Larminie represented the two contending groups on this front. Though Dowden was not among the disputants, the debate was called by Yeats "the Dowden controversy" because it had been started by his remarks at the Ferguson lecture.[40] From these articles, one recognizes that the argument was characterized by three aspects which correspond to the three basic tendencies of the movement itself: nationalism versus cosmopolitanism, Nationalists versus Unionists, esoteric idealism versus objective idealism. To all, nationalism in literature meant the revival of Celtic legend and myth as the subjects for poetry, painting, song, and story, as well as the glorification of Ireland and its heritage; and, to some, it also meant a revival of the Celtic language.

Naturally, an emphasis on nationalism, even in literature, was an indirect statement of dissatisfaction with the sovereign nation of a subject people whose cry for independence found various excuses for existence. With AE, the need for freedom was based in part on what he considered to be the inferior literature produced by the English—a literature "more sympathetic with actual beings than with ideal types," and, hence, one which "cannot help us much." English writers lacked a fundamental philosophy, he wrote in the essay which he contributed to the controversy, "Nationality and Cosmopolitanism in Literature"; they were "content to take man, as he seems to be for the moment, rather than as the pilgrim of eternity—as one who is flesh today but who may hereafter grow divine, and who may shine at last like the stars of the morning, triumphant among the sons of God." [41] Involvement with the actual, AE implies, deters one in his progress towards complete absorption in the divine. With Yeats, the realization of his dream Ireland meant in part the demise of science and industry, which he identified with England. With George Moore, the need for a revival of the Celtic language was the inability of the English language to express adequately the rhythms and magic of Irish thought. With Catholic revivalists, Irish freedom meant religious freedom. With militant Nationalists, it meant political freedom and self-government.

The basic difference between the Dowden and the Renaissance supporters is somewhat blurred by its being cast at that time as a "Nationalist-cosmopolitan" controversy. Dowden, Eglinton, Larminie, and others, who represented the "cosmopolitan" side of the controversy, could not be described either as anti-Irish or as pro-British; they considered themselves to be "Anglo-Irish," men who respected nationalism as "a perfectly natural and genuine sentiment," but who felt that it did not take into account the facts in modern Ireland, whose culture was as deeply rooted in English as in Irish soil. The Anglo-Irish contended that even the Nationalists had in mind that attribution of nationality which had "its nucleus in the Anglo-Irish population rather than in the peasant hinterland." [42] "It was possible to be a good Irishman and yet not to feel in oneself a much greater difference from an Englishman than an Englishman of Lancashire feels from one of Devon," Eglinton argued. "Such Irishmen had come to be called by what was meant to be the opprobrius [sic] name of 'West Briton,' but they might retort that Irish nationalism itself had something in common with provincialism." [43] National literature to this group was justifiable, not as an expression of antipathy to the nation with which they were culturally tied, but only as a sincere native interest in life in general with varying challenges. Celtic literature did not adequately reflect the times nor the life of the whole people; therefore, its provinciality caused its rejection by the cosmopolitans.

In defense of a national literature, Yeats cited Ibsen's, Wagner's, and Goethe's use of national materials. Eglinton retorted that the Continental writers had used national themes not to revive a dead culture, as Yeats did, but in a new way to record the awakening of their own age to new ideas.[44] Yeats's rejoinder was that art which expressed its age and the facts of contemporary life was "not the poetry of 'the seer,' nor was it a spiritual force, for a spiritual force is as immaterial and as imperceptible as the falling of dew or as the greyness of dawn." "Why, too," he asked,

should Mr. John Eglinton, who is a profound transcendentalist, prefer a poetry which is, like all the lusts of the market place, "an expression of its age" and of "the facts of life," the very phrases of the utilitarian criticism of the middle century—to a poetry which seeks to express great passions that are not in nature, though "the real appearance of nature" awakens them; "ideas" that "lie burningly on the divine hand," as Browning calls them, "the beauty that is beyond the grave," as Poe calls them? . . . I believe that the renewal of belief, which is the great movement of our time, will more and more liberate the arts from "their age" and from life, and leave them more and more free to lose themselves in beauty, and to busy themselves, like all the great poetry of the past and like religions of all times, with "old faiths, myths, dreams" the accumulated beauty of the ages. I believe that all men will more and more reject the opinion that poetry is "a criticism of life," and be more and more convinced that it is a revelation of a hidden life. . . .[45]

We are, it may be, at the crowning crisis of the world, at the moment when man is about to ascend, with his arms full of the wealth he has been so long gathering: the stairway he has descended from the first days. . . . The arts are, I believe, about to . . . lead us back upon our journey by filling our thoughts with the essences of things, and not with things.[46]

In a somewhat condescending tone, Russell suggested that Eglinton's lack of sympathy with Yeats's and Russell's kind of art might be caused by his unfamiliarity with the

transcendental philosophy which Mr. Yeats, in common with an ever-increasing number of thoughtful men, has adopted to which the spirit in man is not a product of nature, but antecedes nature, and is above it as sovereign, being of the very essence of that spirit which breathed on the face of the waters, and whose song, flowing from the silence as an incantation, summoned the stars into being out of chaos. To regain that spiritual consciousness with its untrammelled ecstasy, is the hope of every mystic. That ecstasy is the poetic passion; it is not of nature, though it may breathe within it, and use it, and transform its images by a magical power. To liberate art from life is simply to absolve it from the duty laid upon it by academic critics of representing only what is seen, what is heard, what is felt, what is thought by man in his normal—that is, his less exalted, less spiritual moments, when he is least truly himself. Though he has been for a hundred years absorbed in the lust of the flesh, the lust of the eye, and the pride of life, in the moment he has attained to spiritual wisdom and ecstasy, he has come to his true home, to his true self, to that which shall exist when the light of the sun shall be dark and the flocks of stars withdrawn from the fields of heaven. The art which is inspired by the Holy Breath must needs speak of things which have no sensuous existence, of hopes all unearthly, and fires of which the colours of day are only shadows.[47]

The truth, however, was that Eglinton *did* understand Yeats's type of Transcendental philosophy but preferred his own. Eglinton held that, if Transcendental realities be not found existent "in the normal human consciousness, they do not exist in 'poetry, music, and painting,' or at all." [48] A striking passage in Eglinton's article, "Mr. Yeats and Popular Poetry," reveals in a unique manner the root of the disagreement between the contending groups:

The facts of life with which poetry is concerned are not the complex and conventional facts, but the simple and universal. This age cannot have a realistic poet, as it fondly dreams, because poetry is ideal and not realistic. The kinematograph, the bicycle, electric tramcars, labour-saving contrivances, etc., are not susceptible of poetic treatment, but are, in fact, themselves the poetry, not without a kind of suggestiveness, of a scientific age, with which the poetry of Greek and Hebrew tradition vainly endeavors to vie. It is no wonder that an age which has achieved this concrete type of poetry should be content with an attitude of simple politeness toward those dreamers who walk with their heads in a cloud of vision: we can understand its being so better than we can its genial invitations to our poetic dreamers to apply their visionary faculty and quaint rhythmic trick to a treatment of the mechanical triumphs of modern life, as Homer treated the manners and customs of an heroic age. The epics of the present are the steam-engine and the dynamo, its lyrics the kinematograph, phonograph, etc., and these bear with them the hearts of men as the Iliad and Odyssey of former days uplifted the youth of antiquity, or as the old English ballads expressed the mind of a nation in its childhood. When the poetic and mythopoeic faculty deserted the disillusioned Greeks they began to speculate on the nature of poetry, and when the moderns, perceiving a certain void in their lives, have begun to ask for an ideal poetic art springing directly out of modern life, it has been found necessary to investigate the origin and nature of poetry. The further these investigations are carried, the greater confirmation will that theory of poetry receive which is so honourably associated with the name of Wordsworth, and which has been adopted and carried forward by Carlyle, Ruskin, Emerson, Whitman, and others; a theory for the statement of which we may refer to the fragment prefixed by Wordsworth to the "Excursion." It is to give the cause of idealism into the hands of Philistines to allow for a moment that poetry is less a "fact of life" than business or engine-screeching. Far better fall into a ridiculous attitude of hostility toward modern tendencies, like Ruskin or the grim Carlyle, who refused to consider as poetry what was not rooted in the facts of life, or to regard such facts of life as could not be illustrated by poetry as other than "phantasms." [49]

This bold belief asserts that the "kinematograph, the bicycle, electric tramcars" are not subjects for poetry but are poetry itself; moreover, poetry other than the epic of the "steam-engine and the dynamo," or the lyric of the kinematograph, cannot expect to win and uplift the hearts of the people of modern times. This bold assertion, says Eglinton, is "honourably associated with the name of Wordsworth." What makes the Wordsworthian poetic theory "right," he writes a few pages later, is its "higher seriousness and more universal appeal," its concern with the facts of life, and its inspiration of faith and hope: "It expresses its age better and what is best in the age." [50] Thus, Eglinton, like Dowden, the two most outstanding "cosmopolitans," expressed their personal affinity with Wordsworthian thought.

The Yeatses, on the other hand, were not admirers either of Wordsworth or of his thought. To both the elder and the younger Yeats, Wordsworth was, despite his genius, a "flat and heavy" poet, "a clumsy humbug," and "a dull dog." [51] W.B. objected that Wordsworth was an "impure artist" who mixed up popular morality with his work—"the things dull temperaments can understand." [52] The Yeatses opposed Wordsworth's "moral sense" and his exaltation of reason to a position equal to that of intuition in the imaginative process. [53] On these same grounds J. B. Yeats had early objected to Dowden's viewpoint. [54]

Differing from the view of the Yeatses, Russell's opinion of Wordsworth was mixed: he approved the mystical aspect of Wordsworthianism, its divination of a spiritual presence in nature; yet he believed it more important for the poet to draw his figures from the ideal than from the actual world. In the "ideal world" the "dreams, antiquities, traditions, once actual, living and historical, have passed from the world of sense into the world of memory and thought . . . from earth to heaven . . . and now each dream, heroism, or beauty has laid itself nigh the divine power it represents . . . ready for the use of the spirit, a speech of which every word has a significance beyond itself." [55]

Larminie, in his rejoinder to the Nationalists in the controversy, entitled "Legends as Material for Literature," approached the problem by a discussion of symbolism as practised by the Nationalists, particularly by Yeats as influenced by the French Symbolists. Larminie's charge was that extravagant use of symbols and preoccupation with form are signs of poverty of matter, of the dearth of a common idea stimulating to the whole community: "There are no such ideas now. The poets either have nothing to write about, or, if they have, they sit down to their work in a cold-blooded languor from which great results can by no possibility spring. Under these circumstances they naturally attribute extravagant importance to form, and endeavor to conceal poverty of matter by elegance of dress." [56] A remedy for such decadence, Larminie proposed, is a Transcendental faith which may become the substance of art. Not any Transcendental sentiment would do, however, but only that variety which would "accept the conditions" of men's physical plane. The artist must study life as it is, for "knowledge of life and its facts is simply a knowledge of the behavior of spirits immersed in matter under very varied conditions. The actions of men are the chief revelation to us of the nature of spiritual beings under the particular limitations and disadvantages entailed by the physical envelope."

The controversy as it thus appeared in the *Daily Express* has been presented at some length because its articles help to clarify Dowden's position about the Renaissance writers. Then, too, Eglinton and Larminie, as "cosmopolitans," justly represent Dowden's own viewpoint. Exception must be made, however, to Larminie's belief that the spirit of man is limited "by the physical envelope"; Dowden's Transcendental affinities demand the necessity of the one to the other.

Eglinton, Dowden, Yeats, and Russell, as has been observed, were idealists who see the Many as One, a "multitudinous unity which is God and Nature and Man." [57] Each sees every atom of the universe as pregnant with the infinite. But, with Yeats and Russell, the finite reflects the infinite, hence the superiority of the infinite. With Eglinton and Dowden, on the other hand, the finite and the infinite are one; each retains its autonomy, and neither exists apart from the other. With Yeats and Russell, truth is static, to be drawn from the great memory of the world by the mystic-poet; to them, reality can be apprehended with closed eyes.

Not so, however, with Eglinton and Dowden, who would not only insist that truth *is,* but at the same time would hold that truth *is becoming.* The objective correlative of truth is men's striving towards its realization. In a letter to Eglinton in 1897, Dowden said of AE's poetry: "I do not know that we should expect much progress in such art as his. One who has found the secret doesn't need to grow in the common way of growth." [58] The "cosmopolitans" objected, therefore, to a literature which failed to reflect the age—which failed to absorb into itself science and politics, philosophy and morality. A poet does not, indeed cannot, find truth and beauty in other than the concrete present, which is the embodiment of the past and the promise of the future.

The controversy between Nationalists and cosmopolitans is in some respects a new front in an old battle, one waged previously under the banners of Classicist and Romanticist. The Romantics deliberately sought folklore, Nationalism, and other worlds than this one; moreover, they stressed intensity of experience and believed in inspiration and revelation. They were the esthetes "inspired by the Holy Breath" who "speak of things which have no sensuous existence, of hopes all unearthly, and fires of which the colours of day are only shadows." [59] The Classicists, on the other hand, elevated reason, emphasized order and the universal, and exalted the importance of form and respected restraint. The literature they approved was deliberately edifying, self-controlled, sometimes austere.

Under the banner of the Romantics, Irish Nationalists, like Yeats and Russell, could rally; but the cosmopolitans, like Dowden, could not completely identify with either the Romantics or the Classicists. Their position was medial; and, in an attempt to be true to the truth inherent in each faction, their position emphasized at once freedom and form, the individual and the universal, intuition and reason, the infinite and the finite. Such truth is not limited to any one nationality; hence, the name "cosmopolitan" attached to their position. Their "native land" was the good, noble, and beautiful; and it was confined to no particular province or country.

During the last week in February, 1895, a debate on the "Revival of Irish Literature" took place at a meeting of the College Historical Society with Dowden presiding. At the close, he gave an elaborate speech which appeared to have been prepared in advance as an answer to the charges against his unfriendly attitude towards the new Irish movement. The most important passage in the speech, as reported in the Saturday *Herald,* was his definition of an Irish national literature: (1) it must be based on the old Celtic literature and legends; (2) it must come from the Celtic people of the country; (3) it must have the basis and inspiration of a race and racial tradition; (4) it must not and cannot be divorced from the philosophy, influence, and inspiration of the Roman Catholic religion. Clearly, Dowden employed a *reductio ad absurdum* against Irish national literature; for he did not believe it possible for contemporary man to revive an older culture in its pristine significance, nor did he believe in the literary ability of the peasants in the hinterland nor in a uniquely Celtic racial tradition isolated from outside influence.

In the speech, Dowden also purportedly ridiculed W. B. Yeats's list of "Thirty Irish Books" which Yeats had published in Wednesday's *Daily Express.* Dowden pointed out that all of the books on Yeats's list had been produced during the nineteenth century and a third of them during the preceding decade. He himself suggested that the ten best Irish books were by Swift (*Gulliver's Travels*); Berkeley, Steele, Farquhar (*The Beaux's Stratagem*); Sterne (*Tristram Shandy*), Sheridan (*Plays*); Burke (*American War*); Goldsmith (*Vicar of Wakefield*); and Lecky (Irish Volumes of *History of England in the Eighteenth Century*). He argued that these authors were not only Irish in temperament but that their Irish nature was evident in their works, which are rooted in the respective cultural milieu of their day with its attendant values and problems. Clearly, his selection of Irish authors supports his theory that literature becomes great not only as it emanates from the life of its times but also as it has universal appeal.

IV *Conclusion*

Throughout this study the aim has been to point out the relation of Dowden's philosophy to his literary criticism and to demonstrate the dependence of his criticism on a definite world-view. He was a religiously oriented poet and philosopher by temperament; he was a literary critic by circumstance and reputation. His critical studies—and his poetry—reflect his philosophical insights into human experience.

Dowden became internationally recognized as the most outstanding contemporary authority on Shakespeare with the publication of *Shakspere: A Critical Study of His Mind and Art,* which was published in sixteen English editions and in a number of foreign translations; and because his *Shakspere* evinced a thorough mastery of German materials, he became known also as the unrivaled master of German Shakespearean criticism. His criticism of Shakespeare's works was philosophical and psychological, and its value resides in its tracing the development of Shakespeare's world-view as Shakespeare wrote the plays, an early precedent of the psychological literary criticism popularized in the twentieth century. The title of the study, however, misleads the reader, for Dowden's analysis evidences little concern for the form or art of Shakespeare's dramas. Though aware of the importance of structure in the works of art, Dowden was more interested in the mind of the Elizabethan dramatist than in his art. Evaluated on the basis of the thoroughly detailed contemporary analyses of Shakespeare available since the New Critics, Dowden's criticism of Shakespeare would be seen as considerably lacking.

Dowden was also recognized and honored in his day for his biography of Shelley. His two volumes were lauded by the critics for their careful scholarship and for their contribution of new facts about Shelley's life and works, and they were welcomed as worthy to be placed on a shelf with Boswell's *Johnson* and Moore's *Byron.* Dowden's biography of Shelley remained unchallenged as the definitive life of Shelley for half a century. Dowden's biographies on Southey, Browning and Montaigne, however, disappointingly lack the scholarly patience and dedication that distinguish the Shelley biography.

Though worldwide reputation came to Dowden through *Shakspere: A Critical Study of His Mind and Art,* and though his biography of Shelley remained definitive until the fourth decade of the twentieth century, his contributions to literature will survive not because of these studies but because of his penetrating esthetic viewpoint in such essays as "The Transcendental Movement and Literature," "The Scientific Movement and Literature," "Victorian Literature," "Poetical Feeling for External Nature," "Considerations on the Criticism of Literature," and in such a work as *The French Revolution and English Literature*—publications in which Dowden to some extent proclaims his own literary objective and values. His poetry, on the other hand, is mediocre. Yet, he merits the title of poet—not for his mastery of the art, which he achieved only in rare flashes of poetic genius, but for his mythic interpretation of man's experience.

In a time when formerly held values were being dissolved, when no new values were felt worthy of communal commitment, and when a new uncertainty and directionlessness prevailed, Dowden endeavored to adjust his world-view not by an escape from the insistent demands of an empirical science, nor by a surrender of the trustworthiness of his poetic experience, but by an acceptance of the validity of both. As this study has pointed out, his viewpoint is characterized by an essential dichotomy and is rooted in presuppositions analogous to those of the Schelling type of German Romanticism, especially as reflected in the works of Wordsworth and Coleridge: the objective and unconscious become conscious in the activity of the mind, and the conscious and the unconscious interpenetrate each other in the state of consciousness. All nature, both conscious and unconscious, is more or less a manifestation of the same Spirit. Art becomes, then, the revealer and the revelation of that essential reality. Dowden's philosophical method of literary criticism follows in the English tradition of Coleridge, who introduced it to the British Isles. Like his contemporary, Thomas Carlyle, Dowden apotheosized that common substratum which united the conscious activity of man and the unconscious in nature into one universal Divine Power which inheres in both man and nature. Dowden's viewpoint, equally dogmatic as Carlyle's though less bombastic, preserves the Romantic tradition in the Victorian era; but it did so with a difference; Dowden's paid more fastidious attention to the assimilation of science.

In its emphasis on the role of the subconscious in the totality of human existence, his theory anticipated in a measure the modern psychological interpretations of literature based on Freud and Jung; for Dowden's concept includes the universal insights of the collective unconscious, of which the poetic sensibility especially becomes aware and for which it provides a prophetic voice.

But Dowden's view, it should be remembered, was always col-

ored by deep-seated theistic tendencies, though they existed apart
from the dogmas of theism. Hence, his criticism is seriously informed by moral and ethical concern. The immoral and unethical
are parasitical deviates from the necessary universal progress towards ultimate goodness, beauty, and truth. The artist should be
true to the abiding law of morality which is inherent in the nature
of life and which must become a part of the physiology of his
work. His art should be not only a mirror but also a lamp. Though
contemporary authors mirror man as little more than a human
animal or a dehumanized machine and though they fail to find
in man the dignity and nobility that Dowden proclaims, that fact
is not to Dowden's discredit but to theirs. By its retention of a
moral law, his view provides a place for the tragic vision that
contemporary authors specialize in and for the truly comic vision
which they have forgotten. His view reaffirms in a new context
and milieu the illumination and wisdom of all the ages of the past.

A master of philosophy and logic, as well as of literature and literary criticism, Dowden cannot be easily gainsaid; and his honesty
in perceiving and recording the givenness of life cannot be easily
ignored. Like Camus, he acknowledged the existence of a moral
law that directed the instincts, a law not to be identified with any
one instinct or set of instincts but to be a standard by which they
are measured. But, unlike Camus, Dowden recognized the logical
impossibility of such a moral code apart from a religious view of
the world. Like Sartre, Dowden asserted and valued the freedom
of the individual; but, unlike Sartre, Dowden would have credited
the accompanying *angst* not to the heavy responsibility of freedom, but to the Existentialist's lack of commitmemt to a Higher
Being or Law to which the individual members belong. He would
have criticized Sartre's (and his mentor's, Nietzsche's) blindness
to the human phenomena of genuine love and cooperation of human beings as a strange neglect of scientific observation. Men
adopt either a materialist or a religious view of the world, Dowden asserted; and to him the religious view answered more satis-
factorily the questions of life.

His theory is a daring attempt to make whole the dissociated
sensibility of modern man by an ambitious synthesis between the
subjective truths of the human spirit and the objective truths of
external nature. The scientific or materialistic method of observation, useful in a measure, does not suffice to discover the inner

moral and spiritual experience of the human personality, he believes. Dowden recognizes, therefore, that the complexity of human experience, the legitimate content of literature, is interpreted neither in a complete Idealism nor in a complete Realism, but in a poetic theory of organicism which includes both. His postulate of reality as an organically structured whole belongs to the general Romantic revolt against dualism and is characterized by a tendency in the direction of panpsychism, like the contemporary process philosophy of Alfred North Whitehead. That which distinguishes Dowden's view in the general stream of Romantic thought, however, is his inclination to speculate on the Oneness of the universe in theistic terms.

Since Kant, men have been waiting for a philosopher who will tell them whether a reconciliation between Idealism and Realism, such as Dowden attempted, is possible at all. In the meantime Dowden offers his solution in terms of a religious affirmation, and "around and beyond what is knowable will abide an encircling mystery."

Notes and References

Chapter One

1. Letter dated July 23, 1874, *Fragments from Old Letters* (London, 1914), I, 105.

2. H. O. White, *Edward Dowden* (Dublin, 1943), p. 6.

3. Letter dated May 11, 1911, *Letters of Edward Dowden and His Correspondents* (New York, 1914), p. 371.

4. Letter dated July 12, 1906, *ibid.*, p. 342.

5. Hester was born in May, 1868; Richard, in September, 1873; and Hilda, in October, 1875. The Dowdens lost an infant son around the turn of the year 1871. Dowden wrote a sonnet to the child: "To a Child Dead as Soon as Born."

6. *New Studies in Literature* (London, 1895), p. 113.

7. William Kirkpatrick Magee, *Irish Literary Portraits* (London, 1899), p. 70.

8. *Michel de Montaigne* (London, 1905), p. 95. Cf. his delineation of a fragment of Comtian Positivism in *A History of French Literature* (New York, 1897), p. 360.

9. White, *op. cit.*, p. 19.

10. Letter dated November 8, 1869, *Letters of Edward Dowden and His Correspondents*, p. 45–46. Also, unpublished letters from Edwin Ellis, Trinity College, Dublin.

11. Unpublished letter. This letter is one of sixty extant letters exchanged between John Todhunter and Dowden until Dowden's death in 1913; the two interchanged published works and made candid but urbane criticism of each other's literary ventures, as well as of that of their contemporaries. Todhunter asked Dowden to read proofs and write reviews for collections of his poems, including *Laurella and Other Poems* and *Poems and Rienzi* and a translation of Goethe's *Faust*.

12. Early in his studies of Shakespeare, Dowden discovered the *Shakspere* spelling for the great Elizabethan which he adopted for the title of his great work. Later, however, he recognized the spelling *Shakespeare* to be as early and as valid as the alternate spelling. Consequently, both spellings appear in his works.

13. *Transcripts and Studies* (London, 1896, p. 267; *Studies in Lit-*

153

erature (London, 1887), pp. 194, 311; *Essays Modern and Elizabethan* (London, 1910), pp. 251, 270, 271, 274; *passim*.

14. Elizabeth Dickinson Dowden, "Preface," *Poems* by Edward Dowden (London, 1914), p. xiv.

15. Letter dated June 2, 1880. *Letters of Edward Dowden and His Correspondents*, p. 158.

16. Letter dated March 5, 1873, *Fragments from Old Letters*, I, p. 58.

17. After being refused in 1883, Dowden offered one hundred and five pounds for the use of Forman's materials, and the request was finally granted. Dowden, *Letters about Shelley* (London, 1907), pp. 83, 89. And an unpublished letter dated August 15, 1885, Trinity College, Dublin.

18. *Letters about Shelley*, p. 138:

> I must express my surprise and interest on finding so much biography of Shelley and Mary in Mrs. Shelley's LODORE [*sic*]. I had the book two years ago, and let my copy pass out of my hands, bought it again a year since, and read it only yesterday.—Why, the whole story of the separation of H. and Shelley in Oct.–Nov. 1814, bailiffs, letters, etc., is here told almost literally. Then there is Emilia Viviani introduced—A vivid picture of Shelley as a schoolboy. And, what seems to me equally certain, a detailed account of Harriet and Eliza Westbrook's relations to Shelley in the Spring and Summer of 1814. The girl of sixteen made love to at Rhyader; separated at nineteen from her husband by the evil influence of a Mother—the attempt at reconciliation by husband foiled much as it happened. Of course the persons are transformed. Lady Lodore has nobler possibilities in her than Harriet had; Lord Lodore is more like a transformed Byron than Shelley. Mary's own character and girlhood gives one side to Fanny Derham (the student and philosopher-girl) and the other (the emotional side) to Ethel Villiers.
>
> I cannot help regarding *Lodore* as an important document in relation to Shelley's life.

19. Not without surprise we notice Dowden citing information obtained from "copies" of letters between Harriet and Shelley, discovered in Dublin by a friend. Concerning the discovery Dowden wrote:

> Amongst the most singular incidents of my book was the obtaining of a number of letters of Harriet's and one of Shelley's, which were lurking in the house of an odd old lady here in Dublin. No Shelley student has ever seen them, and they are of deep interest, but I can only transfer matter from them without actual quotation. The copies I have obtained were made without express permission by an acquaintance of mine who alone has seen them, and

he has pledged me to the most profound secrecy (I have sworn by the Styx and all other fearful oaths) as to my having seen them, and his part in the business. It needed some skill to obtain them —this old lady would throw them into the fire, he says, if I address her on the subject!

20. *Letters about Shelley,* p. 126.

21. Newman Ivey White, *Shelley* (New York, 1940), I, 676–77, note 28.

22. Letter dated February 20, 1877, *Letters of Edward Dowden and His Correspondents,* p. 112.

23. "Wordsworth's Text," to the *Contemporary Review;* "Wordsworth's Prose," to the *Fortnightly Review;* and "Wordsworth's Modernization of Chaucer," to the *Transactions of the Wordsworth Society.*

24. Unpublished letters to Todhunter, dated July 23, 1885, and August 26, 1886.

25. Magee, *op. cit.,* p. 44.

26. *Fragments from Old Letters,* II, 17.

27. *Irish Times,* April 19, 1892. A speech given by Dowden at the Great Unionist Demonstration at Ulster.

28. *The French Revolution and English Literature* (New York, 1897), pp. 223 ff.

29. *Puritan and Anglican* (New York, 1901), p. 6.

30. *New Studies in Literature* (London, 1895), p. 409.

Chapter Two

1. *Puritan and Anglican,* p. 318.

2. Thomas De Quincey, "Samuel Taylor Coleridge," *Collected Writings,* ed. David Masson (Edinburgh, 1889), II, 138–225; James G. Ferrier, "The Plagiarisms of S. T. Coleridge," *Blackwood's Edinburgh Magazine,* XLVII (March, 1940), 287–99; Anna Augusta Helmholtz, "The Indebtedness of S. T. C. to August Wilhelm von Schlegel," *Bulletin of the University of Wisconsin,* CLXIII (June, 1907), 279–369; René Wellek, *A History of Modern Critics: 1750–1950* (New York, 1955), pp. 151–87; J. W. Beach, "Coleridge's Borrowings from the German," *English Literary History* (1942), IX, 36 ff.

3. Frederick de Wolfe Bolman, Jr., "Development Through 1812," *Schelling's "The Ages of the World"* (New York, 1942), p. 23.

4. F. W. J. Schelling, *Sämmtliche Werke* (Stuttgart, 1860), 3:616, as translated by E. D. Hirsch, Jr., *Wordsworth and Schelling* (New Haven, Connecticut, 1960), p. 38.

5. *Ibid.,* 1:43; 2:73; p. 119.

6. Coleridge, *Notebooks* (New York, 1957), entry 189.

7. *The French Revolution and English Literature,* pp. 20, 25.

8. *Studies in Literature,* p. 9.

9. *Poems,* ed. Elizabeth Dickinson (West) Dowden (London, 1914), p. 105. This second edition was published a year after Dowden's death by his widow; it contains approximately one hundred more pages than the first (1876); the added pages contained later poems undated.

10. Elizabeth Dickinson Dowden, "Preface," *Poems* by Edward Dowden, p. xii.

11. Letter dated November 20, 1971, *Fragments from Old Letters,* I, 18.

12. Letter dated November 12, 1872, *ibid.,* p. 44.

13. Letter dated April 24, 1873, *ibid.,* p. 64.

14. Letter dated January, 1886, *ibid.,* p. 176.

15. Letter dated 1873, *ibid.,* p. 63.

16. *Shakspere: A Critical Study of His Mind and Art,* sixteenth edition (London, 1918), pp. 8–9.

17. *Poems,* p. 71.

18. Letter dated August 13, 1883, *Letters of Edward Dowden and His Correspondents,* p. 197.

19. Letter dated November 29, 1872, *Fragments from Old Letters,* I, 46.

20. Letter dated September 30, 1885, *ibid.,* p. 166.

21. *Studies in Literature,* pp. 70–72, *passim.*

22. *The French Revolution and English Literature,* p. 223.

23. *Transcripts and Studies,* p. 116.

24. *The French Revolution and English Literature,* p. 18.

25. *Ibid.,* p. 219.

26. *New Studies in Literature,* p. 38.

27. *Ibid.,* pp. 149–50.

28. *Studies in Literature,* pp. 236–37.

29. *The French Revolution and English Literature,* pp. 48–50, *passim.*

30. *The Life of Percy Bysshe Shelley* (London, 1886), II, 20.

31. Letter dated November 13, 1885, *Fragments from Old Letters,* I, 172–73.

32. Letter dated March 5, 1873, *ibid.,* p. 57.

33. *Transcripts and Studies,* p. 132.

34. *Poems,* p. 144.

35. Letter dated October 22, 1872, *Fragments from Old Letters,* I, 39.

36. Letter dated August 27, 1875, *ibid.,* II, 137; and letter dated February 17, 1873, *ibid.,* I, 55.

37. *New Studies in Literature,* p. 341.

38. Lily E. Marshall, *The Letters and Poems of Edward Dowden* (*Estratto dagli Studi di Filologia Moderna,* VII, 1914), p. 32.

39. Letter dated March 22, 1875, *Fragments from Old Letters*, I, 126.

40. *Transcripts and Studies*, p. 344.

41. Letter dated January 28, 1871, *Fragments from Old Letters*, I, 10.

42. Letter dated August 30, 1874, *ibid.*, pp. 113–14.

43. *Life of Shelley*, I, 319.

44. Letter dated April 24, 1875, *Fragments from Old Letters*, I, 66.

45. Letter dated May 1, 1878, *Letters of Edward Dowden and His Correspondents*, p. 126.

46. Letter dated September 9, 1885, *Fragments from Old Letters*, II, 147.

47. Letter dated June 27, 1875, *ibid.*, I, 136.

48. Letter dated August 9, 1871, *ibid.*, II, 1.

49. *A Woman's Reliquary* (Churchtown, Dundrum, 1913), opposite page 1. This poem is in red ink; all others are in black.

50. *A History of the French Literature* (New York, 1897), p. 377.

51. *Poems*, p. 59.

52. *A Woman's Reliquary*, p. 59.

53. *Ibid.*, p. 22.

54. *Ibid.*, p. 29.

55. *Robert Browning* (London, 1904), p. 264.

56. Letter dated February 17, 1873, *Fragments from Old Letters*, I, 53.

57. Letter dated March 3, 1872, *ibid.*, p. 21.

58. *Ibid.*

59. Letter dated July 3, 1873, *ibid.*, II, 22–23.

60. Letter dated October 5, 1864, *Letters of Edward Dowden and His Correspondents*, p. 14.

61. *Ibid.*

Chapter Three

1. Letter dated July 3, 1873, *Fragments from Old Letters*, II, 22–23.

2. *Shakspere: A Critical Study of His Mind and Art*, pp. 248–49.

3. Unpublished lecture given at the College Theological Society, Trinity College, Dublin (no date).

4. Letter dated April 16, 1875, *Letters of Edward Dowden and His Correspondents*, p. 83.

5. *Contemporary Review*, August, 1866, pp. 535–56.

6. *Transcripts and Studies*, p. 107.

7. "French Aesthetics," *Contemporary Review*, February–May, 1866, p. 306.

8. *Studies in Literature*, p. 194.

9. *A Woman's Reliquary*, p. 4.

10. Letter dated May 1, 1869, *Fragments from Old Letters*, I, 1.

11. *Transcripts and Studies*, pp. 309, 292, respectively.

12. Letter dated September 4, 1875, *Fragments from Old Letters*, I, 140; and letter dated September 7, 1873, *ibid.*, II, 33.

13. *Shakspere: A Critical Study of His Mind and Art*, p. 260.

14. Unpublished note on Freedom.

15. *Transcripts and Studies*, p. 192.

16. Unpublished notes on Goethe.

17. *Ibid.*

18. *Ibid.*

19. *Ibid.*

20. *Ibid.*

21. *Ibid.*

22. *Transcripts and Studies*, p. 287.

23. *Ibid.*, p. 408.

24. *New Studies in Literature*, pp. 276 ff.

25. Unpublished note.

26. Letter dated February 17, 1873, *Fragments from Old Letters*, II, 55.

27. Unpublished lecture on Goethe.

28. *Transcripts and Studies*, p. 234.

29. *Poems*, p. 94.

30. Unpublished lecture on the seventeenth century.

31. Letter dated May 9, 1872, *Fragments from Old Letters*, I, 29.

32. *Studies in Literature*, p. 91.

33. Letter dated June, 1873, *Fragments from Old Letters*, II, 20–21.

34. *Studies in Literature*. p. 100.

35. *Ibid.*

36. *Ibid.*, pp. 85, 293 ff.

37. *Ibid.*, p. 472.

38. *Ibid.*, p. 169.

39. Letter dated August 23, 1872, *Fragments from Old Letters*, I, 31.

40. Letter dated October 20, 1874, *ibid.*, II, 63–64.

41. Letter dated October 27, 1885, *ibid.*, I, 85.

42. *Shakspere: A Critical Study of His Mind and Art*, pp. 27–29, *passim*.

43. *Essays Modern and Elizabethan*, p. 2.

44. *Studies in Literature*, p. 82.

45. *Ibid.*, pp. 293 ff.

46. *New Studies in Literature*, p. 375.

47. Unpublished note.

48. *Shakspere: A Critical Study of His Mind and Art,* pp. 60 ff., *passim.*

49. *Ibid.,* p. 323.

50. Letter dated June 27, 1875, *Fragments from Old Letters,* I, 136.

51. *Studies in Literature,* p. 99.

Chapter Four

1. Letter dated January, 1874, *Fragments from Old Letters,* I, 83.

2. *Ibid.*

3. David Masson, *Essays Biographical and Critical Chiefly on the English Poets* (Cambridge, 1856), p. 27.

4. *Shakspere: A Critical Study of His Mind and Art,* p. 30.

5. *Ibid.,* p. 31.

6. Letter dated June 23, 1874. *Fragments from Old Letters,* I, 99.

7. Letter dated June 16, 1874, *ibid.*

8. Letter dated September 7, 1874, *ibid.,* I, 114.

9. *Shakspere: A Critical Study of His Mind and Art,* p. 35.

10. *Ibid.,* p. 17.

11. *Transcripts and Studies,* p. 93.

12. *Ibid.,* p. 171.

13. *Studies in Literature,* p. 81.

14. Letter dated October 3, 1890, *Letters of Edward Dowden and His Correspondents,* p. 250.

15. *Shakspere: A Critical Study of His Mind and Art,* p. 381.

16. *Ibid.,* p. 382.

17. *Studies in Literature,* p. 118 (footnote).

18. Unpublished notebook.

19. *Studies in Literature,* p. 490.

20. *Shakspere: A Critical Study of His Mind and Art,* p. 21.

21. "Introduction to King Lear," *The Histories and Poems of Shakespeare* (London, 1912), p. 142.

22. Letter dated July 12, 1906, *Letters of Edward Dowden and His Correspondents,* p. 343. See also a letter dated September 7, 1874, *Fragments from Old Letters,* I, 114–15.

Chapter Five

1. Ernest Augustus Boyd, *Appreciations and Depreciations: Irish Literary Studies* (New York, 1918), p. 151.

2. H. O. White, *op. cit., passim.*

3. Boyd, *op. cit.,* pp. 154–55.

4. Magee, *Irish Literary Portraits,* p. 65.

5. *Ibid.,* p. 24.

6. *Robert Browning,* p. 295.

7. George Russell, *The National Being* (Dublin, 1918), pp. 159–61.

8. Other favored places were Central America, ancient Greece, and India. Magee, *A Memoir of AE* (London, 1937), p. 52; George Russell, *The Candle of Vision* (London, 1919), p. 147.

9. Magee, *A Memoir of AE*, p. 42.

10. As quoted by Magee, *ibid.*, p. 147.

11. Letter dated February 6, 1896, Alan Denson, ed., *Letters from AE* (London and New York, 1961), p. 17.

12. Letter dated July 12, 1906, *Letters of Edward Dowden and His Correspondents*, p. 341.

13. George Moore, *Hail and Farewell: Salve* (London, 1911–1914), pp. 10 ff., 30 ff., 320 ff.

14. Magee, *A Memoir of AE*, p. 45.

15. "Introduction," *New Studies in Literature, passim.*

16. *Transcripts and Studies*, p. 94.

17. Magee, *A Memoir of AE*, p. 32.

18. Horatio S. Krans, *William Butler Yeats and the Irish Literary Revival* (London, 1905), pp. 43–44.

19. *Ibid.*, p. 164.

20. Magee, *Irish Literary Portraits*, p. 26.

21. Joseph Hone, *W. B. Yeats: 1865–1939* (New York, 1962), p. 76.

22. Denson, *op. cit.*, p. 12.

23. Letter dated August 6, 1894, *ibid.*, p. 41.

24. Letter dated April 19, 1902, *ibid.*

25. Hone, *op. cit.*, p. 46.

26. As quoted by Magee, *A Memoir of AE*, p. 20.

27. W. B. Yeats, *Letters to Katharine Lyman*, ed. Roger McHugh (Dublin, 1953), p. 47.

28. George Russell, "The Poet of Shadows," *Some Irish Essays* (Dublin, 1906), p. 36.

29. McHugh, *op. cit.*, p. 73.

30. Letter dated May 15, 1903, Allan Wade, ed., *W. B. Yeats's Letters* (London, 1954), p. 403.

31. As quoted by Hone, *op. cit.*, p. 208.

32. *Fragments from Old Letters*, II, 4.

33. *Ibid.*, p. 55.

34. As quoted by Hone, *op. cit.*, p. 46.

35. J. B. Yeats, *Further Letters to John Butler Yeats* (Dublin, 1920), p. 245.

36. W. B. Yeats, *Discoveries* (Dundrum, 1907), p. 38.

37. *Daily Express*, January 21, 1895.

38. Letter dated January 20, 1895, Wade, *op. cit.*, p. 245.

39. Letters dated July 5, 1874, *Fragments from Old Letters*, I, 103.

40. Wade, *op. cit.*, p. 252.

41. *Literary Ideals in Ireland,* ed. William Kirkpatrick Magee (London, 1899), p. 86.

42. Magee, *Bards and Saints* (Dublin, 1906), p. 9.

43. Magee, *A Memoir of AE,* p. 97.

44. Magee, "National Drama and Contemporary Life," *Literary Ideals in Ireland,* p. 24.

45. W. B. Yeats, "John Eglinton and Spirit Art," *ibid.,* pp. 35–36.

46. W. B. Yeats, "The Autumn of the Flesh," *ibid.,* pp. 72, 74.

47. Russell, "Literary Ideals in Ireland," *ibid.,* pp. 45–46.

48. Magee, "National Drama and Contemporary Life," *ibid.,* pp. 45–46.

49. *Ibid.,* pp. 42–44.

50. *Ibid.,* p. 45.

51. W. B. Yeats, *Dramatis Personae* (Dublin, 1935), pp. 94, 116; also Hone, *op. cit.,* pp. 34, 135.

52. Wade, *op. cit.,* p. 590.

53. *Ibid.*

54. Letter dated December 31, 1869, *Letters of Edward Dowden and His Correspondents,* p. 48.

55. Russell, "Nationality and Cosmopolitanism in Art," *Some Irish Essays by AE* (Dublin, 1906), p. 18.

56. William Larminie, *Literary Ideals in Ireland,* p. 60.

57. Russell, *The Candle of Vision,* p. 31.

58. *Letters of Edward Dowden and His Correspondents,* p. 273.

59. Russell, "Literary Ideals in Ireland," *Literary Ideals in Ireland,* p. 46.

60. *New Studies in Literature,* p. 54.

Selected Bibliography

PRIMARY SOURCES

I. Biographies

The Life of Percy Bysshe Shelley. Two volumes. London: Kegan Paul, Trench and Company, 1886.

Michel de Montaigne. Philadelphia and London: J. B. Lippincott Company, 1905.

Robert Browning. London: J. M. Dent and Company; New York: E. P. Dutton and Company, 1904.

Southey. "English Men of Letters" series. New York: Harper and Brothers, 1902.

II. Critical Works

Considerations on the Criticism of Literature. An Address Delivered at the Opening of the Session, 1863–64, of the Undergraduate Philosophical Society of the University of Dublin. Dublin: William McGee, 1864.

Essays Modern and Elizabethan. London: J. M. Dent and Sons, 1910.

The French Revolution and English Literature. New York: Charles Scribner's Sons, 1897. Lectures delivered in connection with the sesquicentennial celebration of Princeton University.

A History of French Literature. New York: D. Appleton and Company, 1897.

Milton in the 18th Century. London: Published for the British Academy by H. Froude, Oxford University Press, 1909.

New Studies in Literature. London: Kegan Paul, Trench, Trübner and Company, Ltd., 1895.

Puritan and Anglican: Studies in Literature. New York: Henry Holt, 1900.

Shakspere Primer. "History and Literature Primers" series. Edited by John Richard Green. London: Macmillan and Company, 1877.

Shakspere: A Critical Study of His Mind and Art. Sixteenth edition. London: Kegan Paul, Trench, Trübner, 1918.

Studies in Literature, 1789–1877. London: Kegan Paul, Trench and Company, 1877.

Transcripts and Studies. Second edition. London: Kegan Paul, Trench and Company, 1896.

III. Diaries

Unpublished diaries for 1870, 1873, 1874, 1875, 1882, 1885. Trinity College archives, Dublin.

IV. Letters

Fragments from Old Letters, Edward Dowden to Elizabeth Dickinson West. Two volumes. London: J. M. Dent and Sons, 1914.

Letters about Shelley. Edited by R. S. Garnett. Interchanged by Edward Dowden, Richard Garnett, and William Michael Rossetti. London: Hodder and Stoughton, 1907.

Letters of Edward Dowden and His Correspondents. Edited by Mrs. Elizabeth Dowden and Miss Hilda Dowden. New York: E. P. Dutton and Company, 1914.

Unpublished letters of Dowden and his correspondents. Trinity College archives, Dublin.

V. Manuscripts

Mss. on Bunyan, Goethe, Emerson, the seventeenth century, nineteenth-century authors, *Shakespere: A Critical Study of His Mind and Art.* Trinity College archives, Dublin.

VI. Poems

Poems. Second Edition. London: Henry S. King and Company, 1897.

Poems. Edited by Elizabeth Dickinson Dowden. London: J. M. Dent, 1914.

A Woman's Reliquary. Churchtown, Dundrum: The Cuala Press, 1913.

VII. Editions

Correspondence of Henry Taylor. London: Longmans, Green and Company, 1888.

The Correspondence of Robert Southey with Caroline Bowles. Dublin: Hodge, Figgis and Company, 1881.

Lyrical Ballads. Reprinted from the first edition (1798). London, 1898.

Passionate Pilgrim by Shakspere, Marlowe, Barnfield, Griffin, and other writers unknown. The First Quarto, 1599, a facsimile in photo-lithography. London: W. Griggs, 1883.

Poems by Robert Southey. London: Macmillan and Company, 1895.

Poems of William Wordsworth: A Selection. Athenaeum Press Series. London: Ginn and Company, 1897.

The Poetical Works of Percy Bysshe Shelley. New York: T. Y. Crowell and Company, 1893.

The Poetical Works of William Wordsworth. Seven volumes. London: George Bell and Sons, 1892.

The Ring and the Book by Robert Browning. London: H. Froude, 1912.

Sonnets by William Shakespeare. London: C. K. Paul and Company, 1889.

PRIMARY SOURCES FOR WRITERS OTHER THAN DOWDEN

Denson, Alan, ed. *Letters from A.E.* London and New York: Abelard-Schumann, 1961.

Magee, William Kirkpatrick (John Eglinton). *Anglo-Irish Essays.* New York: John Lane Company, 1918.

———. *Bards and Saints.* Dublin: Maunsel, 1906.

———. *Irish Literary Portraits.* London: Macmillan and Company, 1935.

———, ed. *Literary Ideals in Ireland.* London: T. F. Unwin, 1899.

———. *A Memoir of AE.* London: Macmillan and Company, 1937.

———. *Two Essays on the Remnant.* Dublin: Whaley, 1894.

Russell, George. *AE's Letters to Minanlabain.* New York: Macmillan and Company, 1937.

———. *The Candle of Vision.* London: Macmillan and Company, 1919.

———. *Homeward Songs.* Dublin: Whaley, 1894.

———. *The National Being.* Dublin: Maunsel, 1918.

———. *Some Irish Essays by AE.* Dublin: Maunsel, 1906.

———. *Some Passages from the Letters of AE to W.B. Yeats.* Dublin: The Cuala Press, 1936.

Wade, Allan, ed. *The Letters of W. B. Yeats.* London: Rupert Hart-Davis, 1936.

Yeats, J. B. *Early Memories: Some Chapters of Autobiography.* Dublin: The Cuala Press, 1923.

———. *Further Letters of J. B. Yeats.* Selected by Lennox Robinson. Churchtown, Dundrum: The Cuala Press, 1920.

———. *Passages from the Letters of J. B. Y.* Selected by Ezra Pound. Churchtown, Dundrum: The Cuala Press, 1917.

Yeats, William Butler. *Autobiographies.* London: Macmillan and Company, 1926.

———. *The Celtic Twilight.* London: Lawrence and Bullen, 1893.

———. *The Cutting of an Agate.* New York: Macmillan and Company, 1912.

———. *Discoveries.* Dundrum: Dun Emer Press, 1907.

———. *Dramatis Personae.* Dublin: The Cuala Press, 1935.

———. "Dublin Scholasticism and Trinity College," *United Ireland,* July 30, 1892.

————. *Essays.* New York: Macmillan and Company, 1924.

————. *Estrangement: Fifty Thoughts from a Diary of WBY in 1909.* Dublin: The Cuala Press, 1925.

————. *Letters to the New Island.* Edited with an introduction by Horace Reynolds. Cambridge, Massachusetts: Harvard University Press, 1934.

————. "Literature and the Living Voice," *Contemporary Review* (September, 1906), pp. 472–82.

————. *Poetry and Ireland: Essays by W. B. Yeats and Lionel Johnson.* Churchtown, Dundrum: The Cuala Press, 1908.

————. "Poetry and Science in Folk Lore," *Academy* (October 11, 1890), p. 320.

————. ed. *Some Essays and Passages by John Eglinton.* Dundrum: The Dun Emer Press, 1905.

SECONDARY SOURCES

Bentley, Edmund. *Far Horizon: Biography of Hester Dowden.* London: Rider, 1951. Only published biography of any member of the Dowden family. Not critical.

Boyd, Ernest Augustus. *Ireland's Literary Renaissance.* New York: Alfred A. Knopf, 1922. Boyd, a younger contemporary of Dowden and a supporter of the Renaissance, gives an eyewitness report.

————. *Appreciations and Depreciations: Irish Literary Studies.* New York: John Lane Company, 1918. Best available source by a contemporary of biographical vignettes of late Victorian and Georgian writers of the Irish Renaissance. *Appreciations* portray writers who favored the Renaissance: *Depreciations,* those who failed to support it, like Dowden. One chapter on Dowden.

Marshall, Lily E. *The Letters and Poems of Edward Dowden (Estratto dagli Studi di Filologia Moderna,* VII, 1914). Pamphlet of a few pages by an admirer of Dowden. No critical analysis attempted.

White. H. O. *Edward Dowden.* Dublin: University Press, 1943. Twenty-two page commemorative address, given in 1942; touches Dowden's literary theory only in a cursory, popular manner. Some biographical data not available elsewhere makes it valuable.

Yeats, J. B. "Edward Dowden," *The Nation,* XCVI (April 24, 1913), pp. 413–14. Brief eulogy, written soon after Dowden's death, valuable only for a glimpse of the relationship between Dowden and Yeats.

Yeats, W. B. "Professor Dowden and Irish Literature," *Daily Express* (Dublin), February 7, 1895. An indictment of Dowden as the representative Irish critic for his failure to support the Irish literature movement and to evaluate critically works by contemporary Irish authors.

Index

167